MAKING SENSE

MAKING SENSE

A THEORY OF INTERPRETATION

PAUL THOM

ROWMAN & LITTLEFIELD PUBLISHERS, INC.
Lanham • Boulder • New York • Oxford

ROWMAN & LITTLEFIELD PUBLISHERS, INC.

Published in the United States of America
by Rowman & Littlefield Publishers, Inc.
4720 Boston Way, Lanham, Maryland 20706
http://www.rowmanlittlefield.com

12 Hid's Copse Road
Cumnor Hill, Oxford OX2 9JJ, England

Copyright © 2000 by Rowman & Littlefield Publishers, Inc.

All rights reserved. No part of this publication may be reproduced, stored in a retrieval system, or transmitted in any form or by any means, electronic, mechanical, photocopying, recording, or otherwise, without the prior permission of the publisher.

British Library Cataloguing in Publication Information Available

Library of Congress Cataloging-in-Publication Data

Thom, Paul.
  Making sense : a theory of interpretation / Paul Thom.
    p. cm.
  Includes bibliographical references and index.
  ISBN: 978-0-8476-9783-0 — ISBN 0-8476-9783-5 (pbk. : alk. paper)
  1. Interpretation (Philosophy). I. Title.
B824.17.T46 2000
121'.68—dc21   99-048748
                                                                                         CIP

Printed in the United States of America

 The paper used in this publication meets the minimum requirements of American National Standard for Information Sciences—Permanence of Paper for Printed Library Materials, ANSI/NISO Z39.48–1992.

For Cassandra

CONTENTS

	Introduction	1
1	Data and Difficulties: The La Scala *Eracle*, Lavoisier's Oxygen, and Various People's Shakespeare	5
2	Structure: Schikaneder's *Flugwerk*, Gilda's Body, and Horowitz's Liszt	19
3	Process: Greek Meteorology, *The Potato Eaters*, and Madonna's "Fever"	35
4	Kinds	53
5	General Rules: The Uninspired Archaeologist and Freud's *Macbeth*	71
6	Special Rules: The Offstage Piano and Elvis's "Hound Dog"	87
7	Conclusions	103
	Bibliography	109
	Index	115
	About the Author	119

INTRODUCTION

> SOCRATES: Accordingly, you are interpreters of interpreters?
> —Plato, *Ion*

This book is about interpretation. Whether what you are about to read is itself interpretation is a question to which we will return. My aim is to present a *theory* of interpretation, and we will see later whether theories ought themselves to be counted as interpretations. But, just in case there's any doubt about it, I want to say at the outset that the statements in my theory are supposed to be *true*.

What is a good theory? Well, if we consider an example—say, theories of reasoning—I take it we would agree that a good theory of reasoning would give an account of what reasoning is and what types of reasoning there are; that it would analyze reasoning into its elements and articulate its structures; that it would distinguish reasoning from other things that are similar to reasoning; that it would show how to distinguish good from bad reasoning; that it would give a dynamic account of the temporal aspects of reasoning; that it would answer questions about what we value in reasoning and why; that it would organize all this material in a coherent way; and that it would show itself to be superior to rival theories of reasoning.

Similarly, I suppose, a good theory of interpretation would

provide a coherent set of answers to the following ten questions:

1. What is an interpretation?
2. What is the structure of interpretation? (What gets interpreted? What for?)
3. What is it to interpret?
4. What is the range of interpretation? (Are critical interpretation, legal interpretation, psychoanalytic interpretation, performative interpretation, and interpretation of a social practice, all interpretation in the same sense? What kinds of interpretation does the theory cover?)
5. What is the relation between interpretation and understanding?
6. What is the relation between interpretation and explanation? (Is explanation interpretation? Is interpretation explanation?)
7. How are interpretations evaluated? (What, if anything, are the limits on what counts as a successful interpretation?)
8. Is there a method of interpretation?
9. In what sense is interpretation inherently plural? (Does the plurality of interpretations imply that one interpretation cannot be rationally preferred to another?)
10. What makes this theory of interpretation preferable to others?

Some theories of interpretation go by the name "hermeneutics." These theories take one of two shapes, depending on whether their aim is to formulate rules of good interpretation or to theorize the difference the activity of interpretation makes to the interpreting subject. Methodology and validity are of the essence in one case; metaphysics and authenticity in the other.[1]

INTRODUCTION

My own theory includes elements drawn from both these approaches, while differing in important ways from both. On the one hand, I shall treat interpretation as a *product* and will formulate rules, in the sense of conditions that have to be met by a successful interpretation. Success, however, might be definable in the absence of a recipe for achieving it. Consequently, the existence of rules for successful interpretation does not imply that it is possible to draw up a methodology specifying how the process of interpretation should be conducted. My approach will be like the first sort of hermeneutics in specifying rules but unlike it in lacking a methodology of interpretation. On the other hand, I shall also treat interpretation as a *process*, one that crucially involves the interpreter both as subject and (in certain cases) as object of interpretation. However, I shall not take the view that self-interpretation involves anything particularly metaphysical. So my approach will be like the second sort of hermeneutics in attempting to theorize self-interpretation but unlike it in avoiding metaphysics.

According to an idea going back to Aristotle, a theory of anything gives a definition of what that thing in general is and, in the light of the definition, organizes a body of data concerning the thing and solves problems generated by the data. On this understanding, a theory begins by noticing a number of data and a number of difficulties concerning those data. That is the way I will proceed: Chapter 1 presents the data that any theory of interpretation has to deal with; it also discusses some mistaken ideas about what should be included among the data and outlines the main difficulties thrown up by these data. Chapters 2 to 6 then present the theory in four parts—dealing respectively with structure, process, kinds, and rules of interpretation. Chapter 2 presents a structure that is designed to fit interpretation of all types (questions 1 and 2), and chapter 3 describes various patterns that the *process* of interpreting takes (question 3). Chapter 4 outlines a classification of kinds of interpretation (questions 4, 5, and 6), in line with the theoretical conclusions of earlier chapters. Chapter 5 deals with general evaluative questions about assessing any interpretation; and chapter 6 outlines special rules that apply only to particular kinds of interpretation (questions 7 and 8). Chapter 7 summarizes our results, returns to chapter 1's data and difficulties, and examines questions 9 and 10.

NOTE

1. Joseph Margolis, "Hermeneutics," in *A Companion to Aesthetics*, ed. David E. Cooper (Oxford: Basil Blackwell, 1992), 192–97, 194.

1

DATA AND DIFFICULTIES

The La Scala *Eracle,* Lavoisier's Oxygen, and Various People's Shakespeare

The orchestra reaches the end of the ritornello. A beat's rest before the baritone enters. But the rest is not silence. We hear a voice. What did it say? Something like "ai-chi." It might be a sneeze. We are listening to a live recording of an opera and there is plenty of audience noise. Alternatively, it might be the voice of the prompter. The recording we are listening to documents a 1958 La Scala adaptation of Handel's *Hercules* entitled *Eracle,*[1] and Eracle's aria starts with the word "Alcide," the Italian for "Alcides," another name for Hercules (see figure 1.1). Of these two conjectures, the second seems better than the first since it takes more contextual detail into account. Of course, even given all this detail, the noise might still be a sneeze; it's just that if it were a sneeze, then its resemblance to the aria's opening syllables would be a coincidence.

INSTANCES

Interpretation enters into this example at several points. We interpret when we identify the prompter's voice. The prompter interprets the words in the score when he gives the singer the cue. The

Fig. 1.1

singers and musicians performing *Eracle* interpret that work. *Eracle* is itself an interpretation of Handel's *Hercules*, the latter being a musical interpretation of Thomas Broughton's libretto,[2] which is itself an interpretive transformation of the Heracles story in Sophocles' *Trachiniae* into singable verse;[3] and Sophocles was interpreting an older myth.[4] That myth, the *Trachiniae*, *Hercules*, and *Eracle* are all themselves objects of interpretation when critics try to make sense of them.

This example reveals the limitations of theories that would confine the domain of interpretation to the past, thus taking interpretation to be essentially historical in the sense that act and object are separated in time. As a matter of fact, the type of interpretation that was first subjected to the theoretical scrutiny of hermeneuts was historical in just this sense: it was the scholarly interpretation of biblical texts. However, as our operatic example shows, not all interpretation is similarly historical. The singer who follows the prompter's cue interprets something as it occurs before him. What is true is that interpretation is always historical in the sense that it *occurs* in time, but not that in all, or the primary, cases the object comes from the past.

Another tribe of hermeneuts holds that interpretation always is—or always involves—self-interpretation. Our operatic example also reveals the limitations of this approach. It is no doubt true that interpreters bring something of themselves to the task of interpretation, and the self may itself be allowed to be an interpretive construct. But none of this is to say that all interpretation is self-interpretation. None of the interpretations in our *Eracle* example has the self as its object.

Of course, the object of interpretation is sometimes an experience. This happens, for example, in the interpretation of art.[5] Michael Tanner takes up the point, with reference to a certain Bayreuth production of the *Ring*:

> It ended with Brünnhilde getting a nuclear holocaust under way (by igniting Siegfried's funeral pyre), while the bourgeoisie dragged on their TV sets and watched the end of civilisation as they sipped their glasses of Sekt. Such a commentary on the media-potential of all catastrophes (though the nuclear holocaust would probably defy attempts to televise it) is a point worth making, or remaking. But not, I think, a point to be made at the end of the Ring, where it not only jars with Wagner's orchestral peroration, but altogether deflects attention from it. The grandeur of those closing minutes is something to be pondered at length, but it has to be experienced in the first place, not sabotaged. To eliminate the experience is to give us nothing to ponder on.[6]

Tanner's point is that an audience is denied the chance to interpret if it is denied the possibility of *experiencing* what is an essentially experiential object of interpretation.

From examples like these one might conclude that what gets interpreted is invariably in the realm of the cultural. And there are philosophers who take this line, among them Joseph Margolis: "What are interpreted . . . are distinctly cultural . . . phenomena of some sort, interpretable just in virtue of their having cultural features or because they are treated as having such features or because they have features sufficiently like cultural features to warrant being similarly treated."[7]

CHAPTER ONE

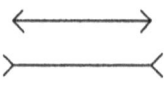

Fig. 1.2

Margolis posits a dualism between physical objects (which have determinate properties, natures) and artworks (which do not have determinate properties, are culturally emergent and have histories), and restricts interpretation to the latter.

Other philosophers believe that nature as well as culture gets interpreted, and if you are one of these, you may find it hard to accept that when we interpret nature, we treat it as "sufficiently like [culture] to warrant being similarly treated." Consider the following words of the great chemist Lavoisier:

> I have deduced all these explanations from a single principle, that pure air, vital air, is composed of a particular principle belonging to it and forming its base, and that I have named *principe oxygine*, combined with the matter of fire and heat. Once this principle is admitted, the chief difficulties of chemistry seemed to fade and dissipate, and all the phenomena were explained with an astonishing simplicity.[8]

"Dissipation of difficulties," "explanation of phenomena," "deduction from a single principle," "astonishing simplicity"— this sounds like interpretation, but not because Lavoisier views nature on the model of culture. One might equally well say that cultural critics mimic the language of scientific explanation. However, there is no need to say either of these things. We need only observe, as we enumerate the data for which our theory has to account, that things interpreted embrace both culture and nature.

There is a second sense in which interpretation's domain embraces both culture and nature, at least according to one view. On this view, it is not just interpretation's objects but its very operation that occurs in nature, namely, in the natural processes of perception. This view is nicely expressed by Jerry Fodor in his discussion of the Muller-Lyer illusion (figure 1.2).

The textbook story goes like this: when the arrow heads bend in (top) the figure is unconsciously interpreted in three-dimensional projection as a convex corner with its edge emerging toward the viewer from the picture plane. Conversely, when the arrow heads bend out (bottom) the figure is unconsciously interpreted in three-dimensional projection as a concave corner with its edge receding from the viewer. It follows that the center line is interpreted as *farther from the observer* in the upper figure than in the lower one. Since, however, the two center lines are in fact of the same length, their retinal projections are identical in size. This identity of retinal projection could be compatible with the three-dimensional interpretation of the figures only if the center line were longer in the upper figure than in the lower; two objects at different distances can have the same retinal projection only if the more distant object is larger.[9] According to this textbook story, our perception of the figure is itself greatly affected by naturally occurring interpretation, though this interpretation is not performed consciously.[10]

If all this is right, then interpretation is directed at the present as much as the past; it is directed at others as well as at the interpreter's own self; it is sometimes conscious and sometimes unconscious.

COUNTERINSTANCES AND DOUBTFUL CASES

All these considerations are based on a recognition that certain types of cases *do* constitute interpretation. A theory of interpretation needs to base itself on some such set of recognitions. Equally, it must recognize that certain types of cases do *not* constitute interpretation. We might agree, I suppose, that mere quotation is not interpretation (although a sermon beginning with a quotation might turn into an interpretation of it). Similarly, an allusion is not, as such, an interpretation. Again, merely to repeat something is not to interpret it. And, I suppose, perversions, parodies, and pastiches are not interpretations—at least, not good interpretations. Other types of cases may leave us uncertain. Is variation a type of interpretation? Or musical development? And what about summaries, restatements, condensations, abridgments, synopses, reworkings, compilations, resumés, and distillations? We shall return to these questions.

PRINCIPLES

I shall be guided by two principles concerning interpretation. The first is the principle of pluralism: one and the same thing can have many different successful interpretations. What this principle amounts to is that in the operation of interpretation, even ideally, the same set of inputs doesn't determine a unique output. This seems to be a basic feature of interpretation. Expressions like "it's a matter of interpretation" and "it leaves room for interpretation" are commonly understood as indicating that where interpretation is appropriate, more than one successful interpretation is possible. It may be that in the scientific interpretation of nature or other special cases, interpretations of the same data ideally converge on a single result. But in the area of the performing arts, where many works are constructed precisely to be interpreted, pluralism is apparent. Therefore, a general theory of interpretation should adopt pluralism, not in the sense that it declares that whenever interpretation occurs, multiple interpretations are possible, but in the sense that in general it does not rule out multiple interpretations.

There are two distinct groups of philosophers who seem to reject pluralism and adopt the opposite principle, which we may name DIDO (different interpretation, different object). In one group there are those who think that, even though the object might be open to many interpretations, *one* of these must be best, so that DIDO holds at least ideally. E. D. Hirsch is one such; but even granting his doctrine that the interpreter's task is "to guess what the author meant"[11]—with its attendant assumption that the author can have meant only one thing—this position has plausibility only in relation to those artworks that are created to transmit a single message. It is not plausible for another class of works—ones that Barthes would call texts rather than works[12]—where the author's intention is to generate a multiplicity of incommensurate interpretations. Nor of course is Hirsch's doctrine plausible for the interpretation of nature.

By contrast with this approach, Robert Stecker thinks that, even though the object might be open to many interpretations, there must be an ideal way of *combining* these into a single best interpretation. He takes as his example the interpretation of Shakespeare's *King Lear*. Surprisingly, Stecker doesn't think that to interpret Lear as senile is incompatible with interpreting Lear as fully in control of his faculties, because "it may be possible that the play can be made good sense of in both ways, so both interpretations could be true at the very same time."[13]

Well, it's true that the statement "The play can be interpreted with Lear senile" is compatible with the statement "The play can be interpreted with Lear fully in control of his faculties," but this doesn't address the issue of incompatibility between interpretations, because these statements are *about* two interpretations rather than *expressing* them. There is a clear sense in which interpretations of the character Lear as senile and as fully in control are incompatible since they attribute incompatible features to the character; and this is equally true of performative and of critical interpretations. Similarly, there is a clear sense in which interpretations of the play are incompatible if they adopt these two interpretations of the character. If this is right, and if there is a successful interpretation according to which Lear is senile and there is a successful interpretation according to which Lear is fully in control of his senses, then clearly two incompatible interpretations may both be successful.

Stecker's view about incompatible interpretations is based on his belief that to interpret an object is equivalent to making an assertion about it,[14] namely, an assertion that the object *can* be interpreted in a certain way. My view is that the making of this assertion is neither necessary nor sufficient for adopting the corresponding interpretation. It is not necessary because there are some interpretations (performative ones) that consist in action rather than in any assertion about the interpreted object, and in general the performance of an act does not necessitate the agent's asserting that the act is possible; when we whistle, we don't thereby assert that we can whistle. It is not sufficient because the *articulation* of an interpretation is not sufficient for its *adoption*; a scholar might formulate half a dozen possible interpretations of a text without indicating which interpretation is to be adopted. The assertions that Stecker identifies with interpretation are merely the articulation of possible interpretations.

Nor is interpretation *of* its object in the sense that it makes a statement *about* the object. Rather, interpretation always offers a *version* of its object. Sometimes the interpreter presents this version as being true to the object; and in such cases, one would be justified in taking the interpreter's actions as involving a commitment to a statement about the object—a statement to the effect that the object is actually as the interpreter presents it. But this is not always the case. Constructive interpretations are not committed to any such statement or to any such truth-claim.

The plurality of interpretations is of two kinds depending on whether a set of interpretations is being assessed one by one or collectively. Sometimes when a single object can be seen in a variety of ways, each of these perspectives claims comprehensiveness. At other times when a single object can be seen in a plurality of ways, no one perspective claims comprehensiveness, but all of them taken together do. In the first case, interpretations are offered singly; in the second, they are offered not singly but in sets, and the object is portrayed as being ambiguous between the various members of the set. Strictly speaking, the members of such a set don't aim at interpreting the given object since they don't aim for comprehensiveness. In relation to the given object, they are *partial* interpretations, though they might be interpretations proper of some other, lesser, object. For example, one might interpret the English word "cape" as ambiguously meaning either a headland or a hooded cloak, and in so doing one would be aiming at a comprehensive account of the word's meanings. If one had simply said that the word *can* mean a headland, one would have offered a partial interpretation. If one had said that on some particular occasion the word is used to mean a headland, one would have offered an interpretation, and one that aimed at comprehensiveness; but the object of interpretation would have been not the word as such but the word as used on a particular occasion.

Stecker raises the issue of what he calls critical monism. This is the question of whether different interpretations of the one object are *combinable* into a single composite interpretation.[15] His answer is that critical monism is correct: "After all, a conjunction of assignments of meaning is an assignment of meaning(s)."[16]

This is right if by an assignment of meaning we understand a statement to the effect that a text *can* mean such-and-such, but not if we mean the *actual* interpretation of the text as meaning such-and-such. Two ways of assigning meaning may not assign a meaning when combined with each other. Interpretation shares some of the logic of possibility. Just as one can't infer a joint possibility from two individual possibilities, one can't conclude to a combined interpretation from two separate interpretations. Interpretation, like possibility, doesn't distribute across conjunction. Unlike possibility, however, interpretation doesn't distribute across disjunction. From any two possibilities the possibility of their disjunction follows; but a pair of interpretations is not necessarily combinable, disjunctively or conjunctively. The idea of interpretation is in this respect unlike that of truth and more like that of a natural kind: disjunctions or conjunctions of natural kinds need not themselves be natural kinds. Swans and koalas are natural kinds, but there is no natural kind swan-or-koala.

So, I do not regard the protests of those like Hirsch and Stecker who, for one reason or another, accept the DIDO principle, as providing sufficient reason for abandoning the principle of pluralism.

A corollary of this principle is that in general when something gets interpreted, it can be identified independently of its interpretation. There must be the possibility of identifying the object independently of the interpretation placed on it; otherwise interpretation could not be thought of as an *operation*—something with inputs and an output.

This corollary is not universally accepted. Some philosophers of interpretation (Nietzsche among them) seem to think that the object of interpretation is always already interpreted. Nietzsche is emphatic: "That things possess a certain constitution in themselves quite apart from interpretation and subjectivity, is a quite idle hypothesis: it presupposes that interpretation and subjectivity are not essential, that a thing freed from all relationships would still be a thing."[17]

Not completely idle. Even if Nietzsche is right in saying that an object of interpretation can't be identified independently of (some) interpretation, it still may be the case (as our first principle states) that what is to be interpreted in a particular operation of interpretation can be identified independently of that operation. So I do not regard Nietzsche as having given good ground for rejecting the corollary of the principle of pluralism.

The second principle that I shall adopt is a version of the hermeneutic circle—an idea that is strikingly expressed by Umberto Eco: "The text is an object that the interpretation builds up in the course of the circular effort of validating itself on the basis of what it makes up as its result. I am not ashamed to admit that I am so defining the old and still valid 'hermeneutic circle.'"[18]

According to this principle, it is not only the interpretation but also its object that gets constructed in the operation of interpretation. We see this principle at work when, in the process of constructing an interpretation, the interpreter makes modifications to the object to fit the evolving interpretation. For example, the sound that initially was heard as a sneeze-like "ah-chi" gets reclassified as Italian "al-ci" in the light of its suggested interpretation as a cue from the prompter.

An even starker example is provided by a remark of Jorge Luis Borges: "Readers create anew the books they read. Shakespeare is more rich today than when he wrote.... Caramba! I don't know whether I dare to confess this—but whenever I quote Shakespeare I realize that I have improved on him!"[19]

Having stated the two principles of pluralism and the hermeneutic circle, I must now outline the main difficulties that our data and principles generate for a theory of interpretation.

DIFFICULTIES

There are three main difficulties.

The first difficulty emerges from the way we have set up the data for the theory. It is the question of univocity. Is it really plausible to maintain that all the kinds of interpretation we have recognized so far can be subsumed under a single sense of the word "interpretation"? Several philosophers voice this kind of worry, among them George Dickie: "Of course, we speak of a musician's particular way of playing a piece as an interpretation, but this is something entirely different and not a declaration of meaning."[20]

Critical, or in general declarative, interpretations may indeed differ specifically from performative interpretations;[21] but specific difference doesn't preclude generic identity. What is different needn't be entirely different.

Gregory Currie voices another version of the same worry: "We certainly use the term 'interpretation' in so broad a sense as to cover both perception and narrative interpretation, and indeed to cover any process whereby we get more from less. But this is a very undiscriminating sense of interpretation."[22]

Currie goes on to put his money on interpretation as explanation by intentional causes. That would be a safe bet. Explanation by intentional causes is undoubtedly a kind of interpretation. It might even turn out to be the only, or the main, kind, but this shouldn't be assumed at the outset. The list of data with which we start should be a risky, not a safe, one. This is because maximum generality is a desideratum in a theory. Currie labels any general account "undiscriminating." But to my mind, a general account is not the same as an undiscriminating one; what the general theorist has to do is to find ways of distinguishing the variety within the unity—of constructing a theory that is ecumenical, not merely eclectic.[23] Currie is of course right in thinking that narrative interpretation differs materially from perceptual interpretation and that both involve "getting more from less." In acknowledging this similarity between perceptual and narrative interpretation, he moves beyond Dickie's purely negative attitude. But this acknowledgment turns out to be hollow, since it invokes nothing more substantial than "getting more from less"—a description that applies to usury and procreation as much as it does to interpretation.

Margolis raises the issue of the univocity of "interpretation" in a particularly telling form with his distinction between two types of theory of interpretation. On the one hand there are theories of what he calls the "classic" type, holding "that interpretation is practised *on* relatively stable, antecedently specifiable referents of some sort."[24]

Interpretation of this type is, in Margolis's term, "adequational."[25] On the other hand there are theories (belonging to "our own time") according to which "interpretation is a productive practice by which an entire 'world' or what may be distributively referred to in that world is or are actually and aptly first constituted (not ex nihilo or by pure fancy but by Intentional technologies, by painting and sculpture, for instance) *for* certain further claims or use, possibly for interpretation in the first sense."[26]

Interpretation of this type Margolis calls "constructive." Such stark differences must surely give pause to those who dream of a unified theory of interpretation. Nonetheless, Margolis himself remains an optimist, affirming that "there are no interesting theories of interpretation in our own time that do not—*or* will not—consider combining both senses of 'interpret.'"[27]

I agree with this sentiment, and the theory I will present, though adopting the classic approach as one of its basic principles, will bring together the constructive and adequational approaches to interpretation.

A second difficulty concerns the compatibility of our two principles: the hermeneutic circle appears to be inconsistent with the principle of pluralism. Pluralism clearly excludes DIDO, but the hermeneutic circle seems to require DIDO: why would interpreters modify the object of interpretation to fit their evolving interpretations unless they thought that different interpretations require different objects?

A third difficulty is generated by the envisaged solution to the first. This is the problem of relativism. If the theory recognizes constructive along with adequational interpretation as two species of a single genus, then it has to face the question of how, in a context devoid of the anchoring notion of adequation, one constructive interpretation can be judged better than another. In the absence of adequation, it is not obvious what could serve as a ground for such judgments.

NOTES

1. George Frideric Handel, *Eracle*, Orchestra e Coro del Teatro alla Scala, Lovro von Matacic, Giuseppe di Stefano Records GDS 3001(3).

2. Winton Dean, *Handel's Dramatic Oratorios and Masques* (London: Oxford University Press, 1959), 417–29.

3. Dean, *Handel's Dramatic Oratorios*, 414–17.

4. Sophocles, *Trachiniae*, ed. E. Easterling (Cambridge: Cambridge University Press, 1982), 15–19.

5. See Richard Wollheim, "Art, Interpretation, and Perception," in *The Mind and Its Depths* (Cambridge: Harvard University Press, 1993), 142.

6. Michael Tanner, *Wagner* (London: Flamingo, 1997), 61.

7. Joseph Margolis, *Interpretation Radical but Not Unruly: The New Puzzle*

of the Arts and History (Berkeley and Los Angeles: University of California Press, 1995), 22.

8. Antoine-Laurent Lavoisier, "Réflexions sur le Phlogistique," 1783. Quoted in Paul Thagard, *Conceptual Revolutions* (Princeton: Princeton University Press, 1992), 46.

9. Jerry A. Fodor, "Observation Reconsidered," in *A Theory of Content and Other Essays* (Cambridge: MIT Press, 1990), 231–51, 241.

10. Fodor, "Observation Reconsidered," 244.

11. E. D. Hirsch Jr., *Validity in Interpretation* (New Haven: Yale University Press, 1967), 207.

12. Roland Barthes, "From Work to Text," in *The Rustle of Language*, trans. Richard Howard (New York: Blackwell, 1986), 56–64.

13. Robert Stecker, *Artworks: Definition, Meaning, Value* (University Park: Pennsylvania State University Press, 1997), 121.

14. Stecker, *Artworks*, 125. He even uses the expression "to assert an interpretation," 127.

15. Stecker, *Artworks*, 114.

16. Stecker, *Artworks*, 140.

17. Friedrich Nietzsche, *The Will to Power*, trans. Walter Kaufmann and R. J. Honingdale (London: Weidenfeld & Nicolson, 1968), sec. 560.

18. Umberto Eco, "*Intentio Lectoris*: The State of the Art," in *The Limits of Interpretation* (Bloomington: Indiana University Press, 1990), 59.

19. Quoted in Simon Leys, *The Analects of Confucius* (New York: W. W. Norton, 1997), xviii.

20. George Dickie, "Definition of 'Art,'" in *A Companion to Aesthetics*, ed. David E. Cooper (Oxford: Blackwell, 1992), 112.

21. For this distinction, see Jerrold Levinson, "Performative vs. Critical Interpretations in Music," in *The Interpretation of Music: Philosophical Essays*, ed. Michael Krausz (Oxford: Clarendon Press, 1993), 33–60.

22. Gregory Currie, *Image and Mind: Film, Philosophy, and Cognitive Science* (Cambridge: Cambridge University Press, 1995), 232.

23. Hirsch's contrast. See E. D. Hirsch Jr., *The Aims of Interpretation* (Chicago: University of Chicago Press, 1976), 34–35.

24. Margolis, *Interpretation*, 21.

25. Margolis, *Interpretation*, 24.

26. Margolis, *Interpretation*, 24.

27. Margolis, *Interpretation*, 22.

2

STRUCTURE

Schikaneder's *Flugwerk*, Gilda's Body, and Horowitz's Liszt

Let's return to *Eracle*. What we are doing, as listeners to the recording, when we interpretively attribute words rather than mere sounds to the prompter is similar to what the singer himself did in following the prompter's cue. In both cases a sound is interpreted as the beginning of a word in a particular language. This operation can be seen as involving three terms—a sound, a succession of phonemes, and a word fragment. It can be seen as comprising two steps—the representation of the sound as a succession of phonemes and the conceptualization of those phonemes as the start of a particular word (relative to a particular language). In the first step, as performed initially by the listeners, the sound is represented as "ai-chi." They can't make satisfactory sense of this in the context, so they try representing the sound as "al-chi." This is also the way the singer represents the sound. In the second step, the sequence of phonemes is subsumed under a concept "it is part of the Italian name Alcide." This concept is also applied to the initial sound. We might say that it governs the whole operation of interpretation. Not any concept will do; it must be one that somehow makes sense of the object.

This example suggests that an operation of interpretation has three terms—an object, a representation of that object, and a governing concept that attributes a type of significance to the object-as-represented and hence to the object. If that is right, then we have an answer to the first question we posed for a theory of interpretation: What is an interpretation? An interpretation, it seems, is a view of an object that purports to make sense of it by representing it in a particular way. At the same time, we have an answer to the second question, What is the structure of interpretation?

Let's now look in closer detail at each of the three terms in this structure.

THE OBJECT OF INTERPRETATION

Whenever you interpret, you interpret something. That something is what I call the object of interpretation, using the term "object" to mean an intentional object. An intentional object is always the object of some act and is identified by the agent of that act via a set of identifying features. From the agent's point of view, the act is directed toward something that possesses those identifying features; and the agent believes that some actual thing does possess them. The agent may also believe that, in the context, there is only one actual thing possessing the identifying features. (The agent may, however, be mistaken in these beliefs.) So the intentional object of interpretation is that toward which the act of interpretation is directed. It is identified via a set of features believed by the interpreter to apply to it, perhaps uniquely in the context. Corresponding to an intentional object there may or may not be an external object, by which I mean an actually existing object possessing inter alia the intentional object's features.

In interpreting the sound that we later identify as an utterance of the prompter, the (intentional) object of our interpretation is that sound; but, considered precisely as the object of our interpretation, the sound is indeterminate in various ways. It is neither determinately a sneeze nor determinately a prompt. Objects of interpretation, being identified via sets of features, are always somewhat indeterminate (but, as Margolis notes, "determinable by interpretation").[1] The score of the opera doesn't settle all questions about how to perform it. The picture doesn't tell you how to look at it. The poem doesn't tell you how to read it. In general, works of art don't tell you what to make of them. Similarly, if you see the night sky as just so many specks of light, then you won't know what to make of it. The external object is, as it turns out, the prompter's utterance, which inter alia possesses all the intentional object's features, along with other, more determinate features.

I don't suppose that the object of an interpretation is itself free of interpretation; on the contrary, it may itself be an interpretation of a further object. The singers and musicians who interpret *Eracle* are interpreting a text that is itself an interpretation of another object (Handel's *Hercules*), and the interpretation they present to the audience is itself inevitably an object of further interpretation. "Object" and "interpretation" are correlative terms; and the general theory of interpretation should not assume that all, or any, objects of interpretation are specifiable independently of all interpretation. As F. H. Bradley put it: "We have, I should say, the aspect of datum, and we have the aspect of interpretation or construction. . . . And why, I ask, for the intelligence must there be datum without interpretation any more than interpretation without datum?"[2]

At the same time, it is clear that two interpretations can have the same object, as when different companies interpret the same opera differently.

Local and Global Objects

When the object of interpretation has parts whose interpretation contributes to the interpretation of the whole, we should distinguish the local interpretation of those parts from the global interpretation of the whole—the actors' interpretation of particular scenes or particular characters as distinct from their interpretation of the play. Some local interpretations are specific to time-slices of the global object (interpretation of particular scenes), and some run through the whole of it (interpretation of particular characters).

The interpretation of a single word standardly requires that it be seen as part of a larger whole, as Schleiermacher noted in his second canon of interpretation: "The meaning of any word in a given passage must be determined according to its coexistence with the words that surround it."[3] These larger linguistic wholes include

> a very complex and undifferentiated set of relevant factors, starting with the words that surround the crux and expanding to the entire physical, psychological, social, and historical milieu in which the utterance occurs. We mean the traditions and conventions that the speaker relies on, his attitudes, purposes, kind of vocabulary, relation to his audience, and we may mean a great many other things besides.[4]

This notion of absorbing the object into a larger whole is not intended to countenance arbitrary additions to the object. Not every way of absorbing the object of interpretation into a larger whole makes it interpretable. The object and its context must be drawn together under a unifying concept.

It is an important feature of global interpretations that they are not simply the sum of several local interpretations. When the actors have interpretations of each scene, and of each character, it doesn't follow that they have an interpretation of the play. In order for there to be a global interpretation, there has to be a single act of interpretation directed at the global object, an act that embraces all the acts of local interpretation. The enrichment of the various local parts does not of itself constitute an interpretive enrichment of the global object; what is needed is a single enrichment of the global object that forges a unified whole. On the other hand, the various local interpretations may be made in the light of

STRUCTURE

the global interpretation, there being an interaction between local and global levels.

Consider scene 16 of Mozart's opera *The Magic Flute*. Schikaneder's stage direction for the scene begins: "Die drei Knaben kommen in einem mit Rosen bedeckten Flugwerk." Any interpretation of the scene depends on an interpretation of these words. In a traditional production, the Three Boys would enter in a machine decked with flowers that descends from the flies. Such an interpretation presumably rests on a reading of the words as a directive, binding on all who claim to be performing the opera.

In the wider context of interpreting the whole opera, the interpretation of this scene is local interpretation. Deciding on one local interpretation is of course only a part of deciding on a global interpretation of the opera. And what is a good interpretation of a part may not be part of any good interpretation of the whole. To be good as part of a global interpretation, it would have to cohere with other local interpretations, all of which add up to a unified rendition of the object of interpretation.

Considered purely as a problem of local interpretation, the question of the flying machine can be debated pro and con. The machine can charm, but it can also creak. And there are also differences of opinion about the status of stage directions in general—whether they have the force of directives or some weaker force. However, there are two global considerations that tell in favor of using a flying machine in this scene. One of them is musical, the other theatrical.

1. The rising violin figures in the ritornello at the beginning and end of scene 16 can be interpreted as mimicking the squeaking of the *Flugwerk* as it flies in and out. (See figure 2.1.) Thus, on a literal interpretation of the stage direction, these passages are integrated into a wider interpretation linking the stage directions with the music.

Fig. 2.1

2. Theatrically, the opera is remarkable for the large number of "transformation" scenes it includes; these are scenes in which one set is mechanically transformed into another. Stage directions such as the following abound: "The mountains divide, and the stage is transformed into a splendid chamber."[5]

In addition to these explicit calls for transformations, the stage directions require various machinery effects akin to scenic transformations, including a door that opens and closes by itself (act 1, scene 1) and more than one trapdoor (act 1, scene 5; act 2, scenes 8, 15, 23, 25, and 30). Early audiences appreciated this aspect of the opera: "Vienna, the 9th October. The new comedy with machines, *Die Zauberflöte*, with music by our Kapellmeister *Mozard*, which is given at great cost and with much magnificence in the scenery . . ."[6]

Scene 16 is framed by the entry and exit of the flying machine and is thus a transformation scene. The "magic" in the opera's title finds an eighteenth-century theatrical expression in these transformation scenes. By following the stage direction literally, we thus heighten one strand of theatrical coherence.

It is clear from this example that local and global interpretations interact. Local interpretations contribute to the global interpretation, and the global interpretation is a factor in determining whether a local interpretation is good. When scene 16 is interpreted as part of the opera, there are two objects of interpretation, standing in a part-whole relation to one another. One we could call the local object, the other the global object.

This distinction is in play in Hirsch's definition of an *intrinsic* genre: "It is that sense of the whole by means of which an interpreter can correctly understand any part in its determinacy."[7]

Hirsch's use of the definite article suggests that corresponding to any local object of interpretation is some unique global object, by means of which an interpreter can correctly understand the local object. But it's far from clear that this is true for all interpretation. Scene 16, for instance, could also be interpreted as an example of the representation of children on the eighteenth-century stage. There are different ways of contextualizing the scene. In general, there is going to be more than one way of contextualizing an object of interpretation, and the choice of one contextualization over another will be determined by the interpretation's aims.

CHAPTER TWO

Figure 2.2

REPRESENTATION

Interpretation subjects its object to a noteworthy transformation. The object's identifying features are altered, whether by structuring, by selection, or by substitution, and for this reason I regard this transformation as a representation. Structuring, selection, and substitution are modes of representation. If we foreground certain of the object's features relative to others (thereby imposing a structure on that set of features), we represent the object. Equally we represent it if we select some of its features (thus stylizing its presentation), or if we substitute certain of its features by natural-

Fig. 2.3

ly or conventionally associated features. Thus it is that the object of interpretation gets transformed into the object-as-represented. The opera is given a particular slant or color; it gets cut or altered; or it is given an allegorical reading.

In production, various parts of the opera are cut, and as a result different (selective) representations are offered to the public. Some aspects of the plot may be represented symbolically.

We see these various modes of representation in our examples. Different versions of the Heracles story structure it differently by highlighting different features. Handel plays up the character's comic side, as Winton Dean points out in his discussion of the aria with which we began:

> Handel is undoubtedly smiling at his hero. The key (C major), the gawky gait of the bassoons in anticipation and imitation of the voice's first phrase, the very shape of this much asseverated phrase (downward arpeggios of the common chord), the rising octave scales at "By actions emulating mine," and especially the tendency to repeat each short motive in the same rhythm, if not the same notes, combine to delineate a boastful, complacent, not very intelligent general who yet remains persona grata to his creator and therefore to us.[8]

(See figures 2.2 and 2.3.)

By contrast, the La Scala interpretation, with its beefed-up orchestration, emphasizes Hercules' heroic aspect. Giuseppe di Stefano described the production as "un esecuzione magistrale."[9]

A difficulty arises from introducing representation as a proper part of the operation of interpretation. It is this: Representation itself appears always to be interpretive, and if it is, then any account of interpretation in terms of representation will be circular. This difficulty vanishes as soon we realize that it is possible for the interpreter to represent the object without yet subsuming it under a significance-endowing concept. Recall the listeners who represented what was in fact the prompter's voice as uttering the sound "ai-chi" but who were unable to make sense of this.

CONCEPTUALIZATION

Whenever an object is interpreted, it gets interpreted as something. To specify what the object is interpreted as, is to specify a *governing concept* that draws together the multiple features of the object-as-represented. Prominent among governing concepts are concepts of the form "signifying so-and-so," "aiming to be so-and-so," "representing so-and-so," "expressing such-and-such," and "explained by such-and-such," as well as concepts of the form "is part of such-and-such" and "is really (or only) so-and-so." Such governing concepts may also include a modifier such as "ambiguously," "ambivalently," "ironically," or "in an unstable fashion." In using the expression "governing concept," I don't mean to suggest something that is expressible in a single word. What is required is a conceptual unity. The verbal expression of this concept may be complex.

An interpretation *lends significance* to its object by fitting the object (under a particular representation) to a governing concept. The reason why quotation and repetition are not *eo ipso* interpretation is that those activities do not subsume the quoted or repeated material under a significance-endowing concept. You can quote or repeat something whose significance completely escapes you.

Interpretation is making sense. But sense can be made of something in two ways. The difference between them corresponds to the difference between something's making sense and our making sense of it. Roughly, this corresponds to the two possible directions of the relation of fit—concept-to-object or object-to-concept. In the first case, interpretations are discovered: by finding out something about the object of interpretation we come to understand it. In the second case interpretations are invented: we make of the object something it previously was not. Interpretations of the first type aim to be authoritative; interpretations of the second type aim rather at playfulness.

A play may be interpreted as having a particular representational or expressive significance; an event may acquire significance by being provided with an explanation or a purported purpose; the objects in the night sky may be given a special significance by being interpreted as *really* divinities. I can't offer any general definition of significance beyond this rather loose list. Does this mean that I'm running different things together under the heading of the "significant"? Of course! Interpretation is a loosely delimited field with parts that are linked only by analogies. It can only be defined by means of concepts that themselves are similarly loose: our concept of significance needs to be as multifarious as that of interpretation itself.

Significance characteristically comes about not just case by case but systematically. The elements in significance-systems are rules to the effect that particular items or types of items possess particular significances or types of significance. These rules may state what a given item *signifies*; or they may state what (or what kind of) *significance* the item has.

A language includes such a system of rules. The word "bald" signifies what it signifies in English by virtue of belonging to one significance-system; it signifies what it signifies in German by virtue of belonging to another significance-system. A sequence of actions might be a significance-system: this is why a text can be given enhanced significance by being performed. The word "bald," while not losing its significance as an English word, takes on new types of significance when it is *uttered* by someone in a particular context. It might be a pun, a warning, a distraction, etc. Equally, codes including codes of conduct, styles of performance, and scientific theories are significance-systems. All endow what falls within them with a special type of significance.

Consider Rigoletto's moment of truth as he drags the sack towards the river, believing it to contain the Duke's body:

> Ora mi guarda, o mondo . . .
> Quest'è un buffone, ed un potente è questo!
> (Now, everyone, look at me, . . .
> here you see a clown, and there a man of power!)

The significance of the situation for Rigoletto is that it is his moment of *revenge* on the Duke. Rigoletto's great passion has been the protection of his daughter from unwanted suitors. Rigoletto is in the service of the Duke. Because he believes the Duke has defiled his daughter, he has hired an assassin to kill the Duke. He believes that he holds the Duke's body in the sack. All of this takes on the significance of *la vendetta*, given a certain significance-system that is familiar to followers of nineteenth-century Italian opera.

But Rigoletto's belief is false. When he hears the Duke's voice in the distance, the significance of his situation changes totally. The horrific realization dawns on him that it is his own daughter's body he carries in the sack and that he remains very much under the Duke's heel. As he holds his dying daughter in his arms, he cries out, "*Ah, la maledizione!*" and in doing so gives voice to another interpretation, an interpretation that makes sense of the otherwise senseless death of his daughter by attributing it to Monterone's curse.[10] We understand this changing significance because we understand the significance-system of operatic melodrama.

ADEQUACY OF THE ANALYSIS

We have analyzed interpretation as an operation in which sense is made of an object by representing the object in some way, placing that representation in an appropriate context; and conceptualizing that representation within some significance-system.

Is this account adequate? Have we left anything out? Could two saliently different interpretations be indistinguishable in these three respects?

It seems so. The music critic Harold C. Schonberg finds salient differences between Vladimir Horowitz's two recordings of the Liszt *Piano Sonata*; at the same time, he finds a certain identity, which we could characterize as indistinguishability in respect to the three terms we have listed.

Writing about the 1932 recording,[11] Schonberg states: "The Horowitz performance is typical: raw excitement coupled with moments of delicate lyricism and washes of color. As expected, there are the flashing octaves and awesome technical command. He holds the sprawling piece together beautifully."[12]

And on the 1978 recording:[13]

> In 1978 he returned to the Liszt B minor Sonata, which he had last recorded in 1932 and had not played for many years. His basic ideas had not changed very much. The only major difference is a quality of relaxation from a seventy-five-year-old veteran, as opposed to the more impulsive playing of a twenty-nine-year-old. Now Horowitz is more careful, and some of the difficult sections are tough going for him. Yet the playing has all the power needed for the big moments, and all the musical parameters are perfectly commanded. The Liszt B minor was still "his" piece.[14]

We could characterize Schonberg's view this way: Horowitz's two interpretations have the same object (the Liszt sonata), both represent that object in the same way (highlighting the same aspects of the sonata), and both have the same governing concept ("raw excitement," "delicate lyricism," "washes of color," "flashing octaves and awesome technical command"). But Schonberg also differentiates the two interpretations in respect to relaxation and impulsiveness. It seems, then, that this critic finds salient differences between two interpretations that, according to our theory, are identical in all their terms.

From the point of view of the theorist of interpretation, what is interesting is that this differentiation can be construed as a difference of terms between Horowitz's two performative interpretations. What appears as a pair of performative interpretations of the same object sharing all other terms turns out to be capable of being construed in another, more determinate, way. Instead of two saliently different interpretations sharing all terms, we could say that we have two interpretations with different terms. Here's how to do it. The relaxation or impulsiveness that distinguishes the interpretations can be portrayed as part of their governing concepts. In that case, we have two interpretations of the same object that represent that object in the same way but have different governing concepts. These two governing concepts turn out to be two incompatible determinations of the single more generic governing concept from which we started. Thus, our theory is able to deal with this case. The reason this type of case is possible is that the governing concept of a given interpretation may be specified more or less determinately.

NOTES

1. Joseph Margolis, *Interpretation Radical but Not Unruly: The New Puzzle of the Arts and History* (Berkeley and Los Angeles: University of California Press, 1995), 27.
2. F. H. Bradley, *Essays on Truth and Reality* (Oxford: Clarendon Press, 1914), 204.
3. F. D. E. Schleiermacher, *Hermeneutik*, ed. Heinz Kimmerle (Heidelberg, 1959), 95. Translation in E. D. Hirsch Jr., *Validity in Interpretation* (New Haven: Yale University Press, 1967), 201.
4. Hirsch, *Validity*, 86–87.
5. Act 1, scene 6. Compare act 1, scenes 7, 9, and 15; act 2, scenes 2, 7, 13, 20, 24, 26, 28, 29, and 30.
6. *Musikalisches Wochenblatt*, Berlin 1791 (10 [?] December). Quoted in Otto Erich Deutsch, *Mozart: A Documentary Biography*, trans. Eric Blom, Peter

Branscombe, and Jeremy Noble. 2d ed. (London: Adam & Charles Black, 1966), 409.

7. Hirsch, *Validity*, 86.

8. Winton Dean, *Handel's Dramatic Oratorios and Masques* (London: Oxford University Press, 1959), 426.

9. Giuseppe di Stefano, liner notes to Handel, *Eracle*.

10. G. Verdi and F. M. Piave, *Rigoletto*, act 3. Monterone's curse, "You serpent, you who laugh at a father's grief—curse you!" occurs at the end of act 1, scene 1.

11. Vladimir Horowitz, *Recordings 1930–1951*. EMI mono CHS 7 63538 2.

12. Harold C. Schonberg, *Horowitz: His Life and Music* (New York: Simon & Schuster, 1992), 322.

13. *Horowitz Plays Liszt*. RCA Victor Red Seal 09026 61415 2.

14. Schonberg, *Horowitz*, 343–44.

3

PROCESS

Greek Meteorology, *The Potato Eaters*, and Madonna's "Fever"

Our third question, What is it to interpret? requires an answer that draws attention to the nature of interpretation as a process; however, it would be pointless to try to give an empirical description of all the forms that this process takes. It would be better to identify a protoprocess from whose iterations and fragmentations every actual process of interpretation can be constructed. This can be done on the following lines. There are four stages in the protoprocess; and these stages are defined with reference to the structure of interpretation we described in the previous chapter. First, the object is identified. Second, it is judged to be lacking in a certain type of significance. Third, the object is imaginatively conceived of as falling under a particular type of governing concept that would endow the lacking significance. Fourth, the object is represented, and this representation is adapted and adjusted, with a view to creating a fit between it and the governing concept. Each stage in this process is revisable.

IDENTIFYING THE OBJECT

Interpreters start by identifying the objects of their activity. This they do by selecting a set of identifying features. Such an identification is revisable.

CHAPTER THREE

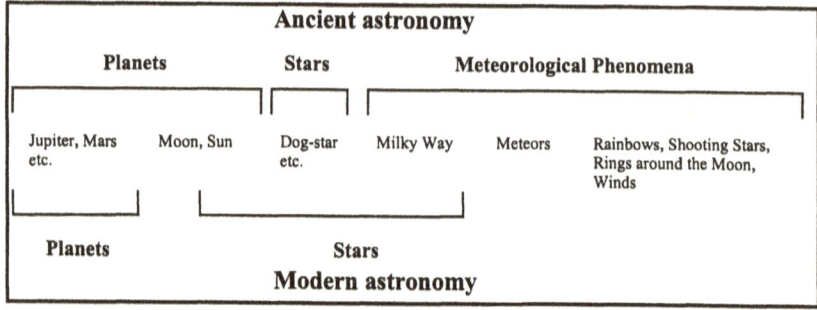

Fig. 3.1

Thomas Kuhn has shown[1] that the ancient Greeks classified as meteorological a range of phenomena that modern science doesn't see as belonging to any single class. (See figure 3.1.) Whereas the ancients lumped rainbows and winds together with what we call stars and planets as calling for a single explanatory interpretation, the moderns have revised, and narrowed, this object.

Interpreters sometimes give up on the aim of constructing a coherent interpretation of the object, deciding, for example, that a text does not admit of a single overall interpretation of the intended type. When they do this, they may segment the text into regions, each with its own interpretation. This move amounts to dissolving a single operation of interpretation into many such operations, each with its own object. As E. D. Hirsch notes:

> An interpretation stands or falls as a whole. As soon as the judge begins to pick and choose elements from several hypotheses, he simply introduces new, eclectic, hypotheses, which must in turn stand or fall as wholes. Belief in the possibilities of mere eclecticism is based on a failure to understand that every interpretation necessarily refers to a whole meaning.[2]

MISSING THE SIGNIFICANCE

In order for the process of interpretation to get going, someone has to judge that the object is somehow deficient and someone has to desire that this lack be supplemented. The person who remedies this deficiency is the interpreter in cases of interpretation-for-oneself, but in interpretation-for-others[3] it may not be the interpreter; Belshazzar is the one who is puzzled by the marks on the wall, but it is Daniel who supplies the lacking significance. It might be that the indeterminacy of the object of interpretation is seen by interpreters as a matter of conceptual impoverishment, and thus as requiring enrichment. To the interpreter, the object's indeterminacy marks a failure, a failure to instantiate a significant governing concept, and what is required is a reconception that will turn the object into something that *does* instantiate such a concept.

Or it might be that the object is seen as somehow mysterious or alien. Thales and the other ancient cosmologists wanted to find significance in the skies. Similarly, most of us, when we see a face, feel the need to find a meaning in it—a meaning that pertains to *us*. And those who think that tea leaves can be interpreted do so precisely to the extent that they think the appearances conceal something significant.

Of course, the process of interpretation may not even begin. There will always be some people who don't *want* to make anything of these objects. Like the prisoners in Plato's Cave who think that the images on the wall are just what they are, these people are not interpreters. A certain type of *desire* is necessary for interpretation to begin, and not everyone has it.

SELECTING THE TYPE OF GOVERNING CONCEPT

The third stage in the process involves the selection of a type of governing concept. The Greek physicists, to their credit, wanted *natural explanations* of celestial phenomena, even if they sometimes looked for them in the wrong places. In so wishing, they were choosing one type of governing concept over others as the basis for their interpretations. They might, instead of trying to explain celestial phenomena by natural causes, have sought supernatural explanations or aesthetic interpretations. Here we have three types of governing concepts.

The idea of a type of governing concept is closely related to Piaget's idea of a corrigible schema as it is reemployed by Hirsch: "A schema sets up a range of predictions or expectations, which if fulfilled confirms the schema, but if not fulfilled causes us to revise it."[4]

To make sense of the object, the interpreter needs to decide what type of significance is going to be assigned to it—in other words, to select a type of governing concept under which the salient aspects of the object are going to be synthesized. At this stage the interpreter asks questions like, What does the object represent or express? What is it a part of? What is it really? or What is its explanation?

When you classify a piece of discourse as an enthymeme, you are assigning a kind of significance to it—the kind of significance possessed by an argument. In so classifying it, you take it to be an incompletely formulated argument and you take its incomplete formulation as demanding remedy by further interpretation. Thus, to classify something as an enthymeme while being unable to fill in its missing premises is precisely to be at this stage of the interpretive process and not to have advanced to later stages.

Similarly, when Belshazzar classified the marks on the wall as *writing*, he thought of them as having the type of significance possessed by a communication because they had the superficial marks of a communication (having been written by a hand). But as soon as it was so classified, the writing posed a puzzle insofar as its significance could not be grasped. Further interpretation was therefore necessary.

Hirsch spends some space discussing this stage of the process under the heading of "genre."[5] He sees genre as something posited at the start of a process of interpretation but that gets revised in the course of the process: "A generic conception is apparently not something stable but something that varies in the process of understanding. At first it is vague and empty; later, as understanding proceeds, the genre becomes explicit and its range of expectations becomes much narrower."[6] (As expectations narrow, however, they may be defeated, and interpreters may find that they have been looking for the wrong type of significance.)

It is important to remember that the governing concept is not always *given*; sometimes it is constructed by the interpreter. It is the mark of major interpreters, in the arts as well as the sciences, that they *invent* governing concepts.

REPRESENTING THE OBJECT TO FIT A CONCEPT OF THE REQUIRED TYPE

It may be that no governing concept of the chosen type fits the object as things stand; in order to achieve such a fit, the object may need to be represented. Equally, it may be that, because a given concept of the required type doesn't fit the current representation of the object, a new governing concept must be found or forged. This is the fourth stage of the interpretive protoprocess; it may involve adjusting the concept to fit the object, or modifying the object to fit the concept, or both. This stage finds linguistic expression in exclamations like "Ah, I see. It's the prompter!" or "I can just see it as a musical!" The object has to be *seen as* the prompter's voice; the object has to be *turned into* a musical. In the one case, seeing involves insight, in the other, imagination—corresponding respectively to adequational and constructive interpretation. In both cases the interpreter's "seeing" appears as something that is not under the control of rules. It is, in Plato's term, an "inspiration."[7]

CHAPTER THREE

Adequational Interpretation

The concept may be fitted to the object. This happens in cases of interpretation that rest on an insight into the object's nature. But even these cases involve representing the object in such a way that the governing concept *evidently* applies to it. Prominent among the types of representation used here is restructuring.

The object may already be thought of as structured in certain ways: its specification may include not just a set of features but also some metafeatures that order or prioritize certain of its first-order features. This structuring may need to be changed if the object is to fall under the chosen governing concept. What had been thought of as primary features of the object may have to recede; other aspects may have to be foregrounded. Michael Krausz discusses an interesting example. For purposes of interpretation, the features of Van Gogh's painting *The Potato Eaters* get structured differently by its different interpreters. To H. P. Bremmer, what is salient in the painting are certain formal features, including the correspondence between the members of the family and their coffee cups.[8] Another interpreter, H. R. Graetz, while recognizing those features as part of the object of interpretation, highlights other features—the direction and expressive content of the subjects' gazes, the wall separating the older woman and man, the name "Vincent" on the chair at the left, the lantern, and the steam rising from the hot potatoes and coffee.[9] These different structurings of the object are determined by the different governing concepts adopted by the two interpreters. In Bremmer's interpretation, the governing concept is "interrelated unity"; this is the significance that the interpreter finds in the object's internal formal relations. In Graetz's interpretation, the gazes and the separating wall—set off against the light-giving lantern and the warming steam—are brought together under the governing concept "expression of isolation." What the example shows is that it would be rational for two interpreters, trying respectively to portray the painting as a formal unity and in

Fig. 3.2

terms of its expressive qualities, to highlight different subsets of its features.

Constructive Interpretation

In constructive interpretation the direction of fit is object-to-concept, and interpretive strategies include correction, cuts, and reconstitution.

The process of restructuring is conservative: it leaves the object's content unaltered. By contrast, the strategy of correction changes the object's features. For example, an interpreter who is trying to constitute an authoritative text might alter a passage in the text on the ground that it embodies an error of some kind.

Krausz discusses an interesting example, which concerns a passage in Beethoven's *First Symphony*. (See figure 3.2.). A literal reading of the last half-beat before the allegro (i.e., playing it in the adagio tempo) conflicts with the reappearance of this figure later in the movement (where it must be played in the allegro tempo), and most conductors choose consistency over literalness here.[10] They play the last four thirty-second notes before the allegro *in the allegro tempo*. While allowing that "no-one suggests that Beethoven did not mean to notate the score as he did, or that there has been an editorial error in standard editions,"[11] these conductors are making a correction to the score, in the sense that where it specifies thirty-second notes they play sixty-fourth notes. At least, they must think that the score is misleading.

Cutting is another nonconservative interpretive strategy. Sometimes interpreters delete or omit part of the object (as in modern astronomy's omission of rainbows from the "meteorological" phenomena to be interpreted). In musical performance, it is common to omit repeats. In the theater hardly a play goes on without some cuts being made. Let's consider an example.

Dennis Bartholomeusz has written on eighteenth-century adaptations of Shakespeare's *Winter's Tale*, commenting that "an attempt was made to preserve the romance and joy of *The Winter's Tale* without its grief and desolation."[12] This type of interpretive move takes certain features of the object to be undesirable and therefore omits them in the object-as-represented; at the same time other features that may or may not be present in the object are taken as desirable and their presence in the object-as-represented is heightened. Romance and joy are the governing concepts that draw together eighteenth-century versions of *The Winter's Tale* under such an interpretation. These are features of the play, along with the unwanted features of grief and desolation. The object, in these cases, is being fitted to the concept rather than the other way round.

The sorts of reasons that get advanced in favor of such cuts may be illustrated by a few examples. Here are three critics writing on Garrick's adaptation:

> Besides giving an elegant form to a monstrous composition, you have in your own additions written up the best scenes in this play. [William Warburton][13]

PROCESS

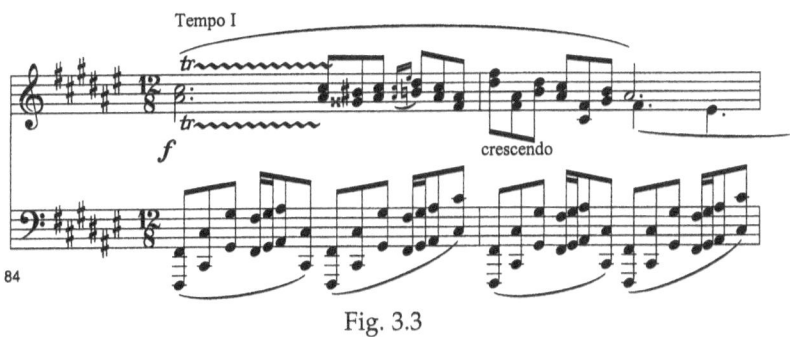

Fig. 3.3

> Without considerable alterations, fine music, gay scenes, beautiful decoration and excellent performers, I would not hazard *The Faithful Shepherdess* upon a London stage in these cultivated times. [Thomas Davies][14]

> It is possible that extended into Five Acts the Improbabilities and Changes of Place would have tired, whereas at present the whole is more compact, Absurdities are retracted, and our Attention is alive Throughout. *[The London Chronicle]*[15]

Elegance, fine music, gay scenes, beautiful decoration, and excellent performers—all subsumed under a governing concept of cultivation—are here taken as the salient features of Garrick's interpretation. They are judged to be lacking in the object (Shakespeare's play), which, on the contrary, is characterized by the unwanted features of "monstrousness," "improbability," "tiresomeness," and "absurdity."

An even more radical type of representation may occur: reconstitution. This may take two forms. Conservative reconstitution identifies an aim of the object of interpretation and reconstitutes the object so as to achieve that aim better. Radical reconstitution substitutes a (supposedly) better aim and constitutes an object that aims to achieve this new aim.

As an example of conservative reconstitution consider Chopin's last recital. (See figure 3.3.)

CHAPTER THREE

We have it on the authority of Sir Charles Hallé that when Chopin, at his final Paris recital (at the Salle Pleyel on Wednesday 16 February 1848), played his Barcarolle, he did so by changing the dynamics of bars 84 ff. from *forte crescendo* to *pianissimo*, "but with such wonderful nuances, that one remained in doubt if this new reading were not preferable to the accustomed one."[16]

Sometimes interpreters—even, as in this case, authors qua interpreters—go counter to what the text requires in the name of improving on the text, while acknowledging the text's aims for what they are. (At least, we may suppose that this is what Chopin was doing.)

Ates Orga and Nikolai Demidenko, writing about this case, take a further interpretive step: "In the parlance of computer software, Chopin's music, as an experience, is 'virtual', capable of being realised and understood in any number of ways, each different yet compatible."[17]

Their hypothesis is in effect that "Chopin's music" is more abstract than indicated by the score; they understand the "music" as not including that forte crescendo. But what about other dynamic markings in the score? And tempo and expressive markings? There is an unclarity about what "the music" is, if the score doesn't fully specify it. On the Orga/Demidenko hypothesis, Chopin in his last recital was following the music of his *Barcarolle*, but this music is not fully specified by the score or by any other publicly accessible criterion.

An alternative hypothesis retains the score as the criterion of the music's identity but denies that Chopin was playing his own music accurately. On this view, Chopin was engaged in a piece of conservative reconstitution. Works for performance need public identity conditions, and it is not uncommon for composers to depart, in performance, from the letter of their own works. Perhaps Chopin was thinking, "Consistent with the piece's general aims, it could have gone this way"; that wouldn't be unusual, since all composition involves choice and thus the existence of ways the piece could have gone but didn't. But this wouldn't explain what he was *doing* in performing it that way. Maybe what he was doing was identifying publicly an alternative version of the *Barcarolle*. In this event we could say that the *Barcarolle* exists in two versions—one as specified by the score, the other with Chopin's change to the dynamics. Or maybe, aware that it was to be his last public appearance, he was not merely performing the *Barcarolle* but using it as an expression of his farewell to public life.

Sometimes in the process of matching object and concept, a focus is maintained on the original object of interpretation. In radical reconstitution, however, the focus on the original object is lost, forgotten, subverted, or rejected; and though the process may end up with a product having the characteristics of an interpretation, it is no longer an interpretation of that original object.

The Otis Blackwell rhythm-and-blues song "Fever" was recorded by Peggy Lee in 1958 and again (in a video recording) by Madonna in 1993.[18] The two performers make something totally different of the song. First of all, consider the music.[19] Madonna's musical arrangement is cluttered compared to the suggestively spare Lee version. Madonna's rhythm marches mechanically, with its thudding disco beat, in contrast to the Lee version, which critics describe as "finger-snapping" and "jazzy,"[20] adding that Lee "is a rhythm singer, who moves all around the beat and swings intensely."[21]

Peggy Lee's voice has been described as having "the texture of a sugared almond";[22] the texture of Madonna's voice perhaps is more like an aging cashew. Altogether, Lee's version possesses a musical eroticism lacking in Madonna's.

But does any of this matter? Is Madonna's version primarily a musical performance? David Tetzlaff doesn't think so. He dismisses the musical element in Madonna's performances: "*Irrelevant* is quite a good word to describe the role musical values play in the Madonna phenomenon."[23]

Actually, the music is far from irrelevant in the construction of her total performance, being the base on which it builds: the choreography and camera work presuppose it and are structured by it. (It's also true that the singing and the musical interpretation generally are pretty basic in another sense.) But Tetzlaff has a point. The music, while well integrated with the other elements in Madonna's interpretation, has subsided to a minor place in the whole. Just as in Gounod's *Ave Maria*—where a Bach prelude is reduced to the status of an accompaniment—it is appropriate here to speak of *reconstitution* of the song. Madonna's reconstitution of the song occurs at two levels. There are aesthetic features of her performance, including the stage production; even at the aesthetic level, her "Fever" is not just a song but is framed by simple and effective staging and choreography that hold the viewer's attention through their clear narrative line and stylized simulation of sexual activity. The song has been conceived as, and represented as, a production number—one in which the music has been relegated to a position of minor importance.

Of greater importance is the performance's political dimension, which is complex. One part of it is carried by Madonna's image as an "iconoclastic teenage idol,"[24] challenging boundaries of the sexually permissible. (Though her "Fever" is so highly stylized that it excludes any possibility of giving offense.) Another political element in her reinterpretation of "Fever," and in her performances generally, is carried by that aspect of Madonna's image, which, in Douglas Kellner's words, "highlights the social constructedness of identity, fashion, and sexuality."[25]

In keeping with this message, there is a high degree of irony in Madonna's performances.[26] Her look at the camera shortly after the start of "Fever" continues a recurring feature of her performances.[27] Kellner sees this gesture as signifying that "Madonna would reveal something of herself in the video, but that she knew that her performance was an act and that she would maintain her control and subjectivity."[28]

Later in the video she winks at the audience, a gesture that is open to a similar reading. Because of this ironic element, it's not always clear what Madonna's political message is. Madonna presents herself (and represents women) as utterly self-possessed, always in control; and some commentators take this to show that her political message is a feminist one. Others take her highlighting of fashion and of her own body as antifeminist.[29] The issue is complex, and raises the question of the very meaning of "feminism," but for present purposes it need not be pursued. Instead, we should query the need for there to be an unambiguous political message. Madonna's performances are art, after all—art that incorporates a play of sometimes conflicting social and political ideas. That play of ideas and images provokes a multiplicity of audience interpretations. While this is bad news for those awaiting a definite political message, it is to Madonna's credit as an artist. Drawing these strands together, we can say—by way of interpretation—that the reconstituted object is subsumed in Madonna's interpretation under a governing concept of *performance*. But this concept of performance is a special one, one that involves self-reference and that is of Madonna's own devising, drawing together elements from gym culture, the world of youth fashion, and Madonna's own performances.

It would be possible to interpret Madonna's "Fever" as an interpretation of the song—an interpretation, perhaps, that passes a sardonic comment on its object. On this view, she illuminates the song but casts it in an unfavorable light. On another view, Madonna's performance is not an interpretation at all but merely the product of a process whose starting point was the song.

HERMENEUTIC CIRCLES

In speaking of these four stages in the protoprocess of interpretation, I don't mean to suggest that in practice interpretation always proceeds from the identification of an object judged to be deficient in a certain type of significance via its subsumption under a governing concept to its representation under a suitable scheme. The actual sequence of events is rarely so straightforward, as Hirsch observes:

> We *cannot* understand a part as such until we have a sense of the whole. Dilthey called this apparent paradox the hermeneutic circle and observed that it was not vicious because a genuine dialectic always occurs between our idea of the whole and our perception of the parts that constitute it. Once the dialectic has begun, neither side is totally determined by the other.[30]

Hirsch notes that in some later versions (he mentions Heidegger), the hermeneutic circle appears as the idea of an "unalterable and inescapable pre-understanding."[31] By contrast, Hirsch—rightly, I think—prefers to emphasize the temporal aspect of the process and the revisability of its terms, and it seems that Dilthey's reference to a "dialectic" would also sanction this approach.

In discussing the structure of interpretation in chapter 2, we took it that the governing concept and other elements were fixed. But in real time things are not so simple. In the process of interpreting, we sometimes find that the object-as-represented cannot be made to fit the concept without substantially changing one or the other. In this case we can try varying the concept or varying the object, adapting one to fit the other. Thus a genuine dialectic arises among the terms of the interpretation in which any one of them may be adjusted to fit the others.

Even the identification of the object may be a process. This occurs, for instance, when the interpreter is a spectator, a listener, or a reader; or when the interpreter is a participant in a conversation and what is being interpreted is the ongoing (but as-yet-incomplete) conversation. Anticipation and predictive guessing play an important role in such interpretation. Halfway through the novel the wily reader guesses the meaning of the whole. The adept listener anticipates the phrase's ending and thus its sense.

ADOPTING AN INTERPRETATION

It is one thing to recognize the existence of several defensible or admissible interpretations—even, perhaps, because one has constructed them for one's self—and another thing actually to adopt one of them. (Imagine a conductor who spends the whole rehearsal going through various possible interpretations without ever indicating which is to be adopted!) For me to adopt an interpretation is for me to make it *mine*. But there are different ways in which I may make it mine. Making an interpretation mine can take place in an *experiential* sense when I experience it as integrated with some set of my mental states. In addition to this sense, there is a *hypothetical* sense of adopting an interpretation in which I recognize that an interpretation *would* fit with various of my mental states without so experiencing it. The mental states in question include my beliefs, attitudes, favored significance-endowing structures, and so on.

Both the experiential and the hypothetical senses subdivide into two cases. In one case (let's call it *assimilative*) I assimilate the interpretation to an "I" that is antecedently determined in some way. In the other case (let's call it *constitutive*) there is no such "I": my self-definition (or self-interpretation), such as it is, does not include the requisite beliefs, types of significance, and so on. So what I do is to take them on precisely as an act of constitutive self-interpretation. The act of adopting one interpretation involves another interpretive act, this time of self-interpretation. In order for me to adopt the first interpretation I must have certain beliefs and attitudes; so I assume those beliefs and attitudes and by so doing partly determine who *I* am. Choosing an interpretation is in this case part of choosing who to be.

NOTES

1. Thomas Kuhn, "The Natural and the Human Sciences," in *The Interpretive Turn: Philosophy, Science, Culture*, ed. David R. Hiley, James F. Bohman, and Richard Shusterman (Ithaca, N.Y.: Cornell University Press, 1991), 19.

2. E. D. Hirsch Jr., *Validity in Interpretation* (New Haven: Yale University Press, 1967), 172.

3. Annette Barnes's distinction. See her *On Interpretation: A Critical Analysis* (Oxford: Basil Blackwell, 1988), 16.

4. E. D. Hirsch Jr., *The Aims of Interpretation* (Chicago: University of Chicago Press, 1976), 32.

5. Hirsch, *Validity,* chap. 3.

6. Hirsch, *Validity,* 77.

7. Plato, *Ion,* trans. Lane Cooper, in *The Collected Dialogues of Plato Including the Letters,* ed. Edith Hamilton and Huntington Cairns (New York: Pantheon Books, 1961), 215–28, 533e.

8. Michael Krausz, *Rightness and Reasons: Interpretation in Cultural Practices* (Ithaca, N.Y.: Cornell University Press, 1993), 72.

9. Krausz, *Rightness and Reasons,* 73.

10. Krausz, *Rightness and Reasons,* 20–21.

11. Krausz, *Rightness and Reasons,* 21.

12. Dennis Bartholomeusz, *The Winter's Tale in Performance in England and America 1611–1976* (Cambridge: Cambridge University Press, 1982), 29.

13. Bartholomeusz, *The Winter's Tale,* 37.

14. Bartholomeusz, *The Winter's Tale,* 38.

15. Bartholomeusz, *The Winter's Tale,* 34.

16. Ates Orga and Nikolai Demidenko, liner notes to Chopin, *The Four Scherzi,* Nikolai Demidenko, Hyperion CDA66514, 1991.

17. Orga and Demidenko, liner notes to Chopin, *Scherzi.*

18. *Madonna:The Girlie Show, Live Down Under.* Warner Reprise Video 7599383913; *Peggy Lee: Twenty-Four Great Songs.* Personality PRS 23012.

19. Phil Hardy and Dave Laing (*The Faber Companion to Twentieth-Century Popular Music,* rev. ed. [London: Faber & Faber, 1995], 548–49) describe this version as "fine" and Lee's singing as "restrained yet soulful" and "subdued."

20. *Faber Companion,* 484.

21. *Faber Companion,* 484.

22. Liner notes to *Peggy Lee: Twenty-Four Great Songs.*

23. David Tetzlaff, "Metatextual Girl," in *The Madonna Connection,* ed. Cathy Schwichtenberg (Boulder, Colo.: Westview Press, 1993), 239–63, 240.

24. *Faber Companion,* 605.

25. Douglas Kellner, "Madonna, Fashion, and Identity," in *On Fashion,* ed. Shari Benstock and Suzanne Ferriss (New Brunswick, N.J.: Rutgers University Press, 1994), 159–82, 159.

26. Kellner, "Madonna," 167 f.

27. It goes back to her 1983 video *Lucky Star,* which opens with her slowly removing her black sunglasses while looking intensely at the camera. See Kellner, "Madonna," 163–64.

28. Kellner, "Madonna," 171 f.
29. See Laurie Schulze, Anne Barton White, and Jane D. Brown, "'A Sacred Monster in her Prime': Audience Construction of Madonna as Low-Other," in *The Madonna Connection: Representational Politics, Subcultural Identities, and Cultural Theory*, ed. Cathy Schwichtenberg (Sydney: Allen & Unwin, 1993), 15–37, esp. 26–31.
30. Hirsch, *Validity*, 259.
31. Hirsch, *Aims*, 32–33.

4

KINDS

The structure of interpretation outlined in the previous chapter is found alike in the interpretation of nature and the interpretation of cultural items, and this same structure is found in performative as well as critical interpretations, in naturally occurring as well as in culturally constructed interpretations. There we have an answer to our question, What is the range of interpretation? This list of oppositions falls short of being a principled classification of interpretation's kinds; nonetheless, it does point the way to such a principled classification.

The interpretation of nature differs from that of cultural items in its objects. Performative interpretation differs from critical interpretation in the ways the object of interpretation is represented; so do naturally occurring and culturally constructed interpretations. Similarly, we could differentiate one kind of interpretation from another by reference to differences in the kinds of governing concepts they employ; explanations differ from critical interpretations in this way.

It seems, then, that in general the distinctions we make among kinds of interpretation can be accounted for by differences among the types of object, representation, or governing concept used by various interpretations.

CHAPTER FOUR

CLASSIFICATION BY OBJECT

The object of interpretation may be a text, an action, or a person; it may be an artifact or part of nature; it may be present or past. Objects of interpretation include dreams; unexplained facts; damaged texts; historical documents; unfamiliar social practices; sentences in unknown languages; works of literature and visual art; unperformed music, drama, or dance; and the conversation of our companions. Another type of interpretive object occurs during the process of artistic creation, when the artist takes a set of elements from the emerging artwork and subjects them to illuminating transformations. The development of musical themes falls into this class.

We distinguish different kinds of interpretation according to whether they have these different types of objects; for example, we are accustomed to distinguishing textual interpretation from the interpretation of art or nature, and so on.

CLASSIFICATION BY REPRESENTATION

When we interpret an object for ourselves, our representing it consists merely in our *thinking* of it under some particular guise. When, by contrast, we interpret it for others, we have to *present* the object under a guise for their consideration. Such a presentation may be linguistic or it may take the form of non-linguistic actions, as when we perform a work in a particular way.

We distinguish different kinds of interpretation according to whether they employ these different types of representation; for example, we are accustomed to distinguishing performative interpretation, wherein we present a version of the object in action, from critical interpretation, wherein we present a version of the object in discourse.

CLASSIFICATION BY GOVERNING CONCEPT

Prominent among governing concepts are concepts of the form "aiming to be so-and-so," "representing so-and-so," "expressing such-and-such," and "explained by such-and-such." Corresponding to these forms of governing concept, we can distinguish teleological, representational, expressive, and explanatory interpretations. The governing concept may be a theoretical predicate indicating what the object is or what it signifies, or else it may give psychological or historical information about the circumstances of the object's production. On the basis of these distinctions, theoretical interpretation (whether natural or semiotic) can be distinguished from genetic interpretation (whether psychological or historical).

E. D. Hirsch distinguishes *interpretatio* from *applicatio*:

> Interpretation includes both functions whenever it answers both the question, What does this text mean?, and also the question, What use or value does it have: how is its meaning applied to me, to us, to our particular situation? The most obvious example of applicatio would be the Sunday sermon that interprets and applies a biblical text, or the legal decision that interprets and applies a law, or the literary essay that describes "what *Huckleberry Finn* means to us, today."[1]

This distinction can also be shown to rest on a distinction between different kinds of governing concept. Hirsch associates interpretatio with meaning, applicatio with significance;[2] and he understands meaning and significance as mutually exclusive: "The term 'meaning' refers to the whole verbal meaning of a text. . . . 'Significance' is textual meaning as related to some context, indeed any context, beyond itself."[3]

But surely, to expound the verbal meaning of a text is precisely to relate that text, identified independently of any attribution of meaning, to a context beyond itself—namely, a lexicon that correlates such texts with meanings. So to allow Hirsch's senses for "meaning" and "significance" is not to admit that meaning and significance are mutually exclusive; on the contrary, it seems clear that meaning is one species of significance. To attribute a meaning to a word, one has to place it in the context of a significance-system, including a lexicon; so if to place something in a larger context is to attribute significance to it, then to attribute meaning is to attribute significance. This being so, if interpretatio is a type of interpretation, defined as the exposition of meanings, then it is distinguished from other types by the kind of significance-system it uses—ones drawn from the lexicon. In any case, both interpretatio and applicatio are primarily kinds of governing concept.

Gadamer takes applicatio to be implicit in all interpretation: "To interpret means precisely to bring one's own preconceptions into play so that the text's meaning can really be made to speak for us."[4] I think he runs two ideas together here. Interpreters inevitably bring their own preconceptions into play in conceiving, in representing, and even in identifying the objects of their representations. But this isn't to say that the governing concepts of their interpretations must include a reference to the interpreter or to the interpreter's audience, as would be the case with applicatio.

CLASSIFICATION BY OBJECT AND REPRESENTATION

Some kinds of interpretation are defined by reference to a combination of object-type and representation-type. I would like to spend some time discussing one such kind—performative interpretation, which operates on a characteristic sort of object (a work for performance) and represents its object in a characteristic sort of way (in action projected for an audience).

You might think, with Jerrold Levinson, that, strictly speaking, performance cannot be interpretation; it can be interpretation only in a secondary or derivative sense. Levinson thinks that it is merely a "curious fact" that the word "interpretation" is applied both to performances and to critical discourse about them.⁵ He tries to explain this fact by noting "that critical discourse sometimes guides the development of a performance; that performances sometimes trigger critical discourse; that performances and critical analyses sometimes originate in tandem; and that performers, like translators (whom we call 'interpreters') are transmitters."⁶

This, I think, is an inadequate explanation. It is better to say that performances are interpretive in the same sense as criticism. The difference lies in the way in which the object of interpretation gets represented: performative interpretation represents its object in *action* rather than discourse. But there are two types of performative interpretation. Not all playing is performance, since performance involves projection as well as execution—showing as well as doing. (And this distinction can be drawn by the audience as well as by the performer.) Performers aim to show only some of what they are doing; the decision not to show all that is being done may arise from a belief that there is an art of concealing art.

Of course, showing is itself a kind of doing, so the question arises for performers whether to show that they are showing; the decision to do so marks a performance as Brechtian. If the showing is not itself shown, audience attention is directed at the content of what is projected rather than at its being projected. So performative interpretation can exist either at the level of what is done or at the level of what is projected. What I do by way of making sense of a piece I am playing may or may not be projected to my audience. Just as some of the conductor's gestures are only for the orchestra, some of the solo performer's actions, required to make sense of the music, are not for the audience to see.

According to Levinson the relation between a performance and the performer's analytical or critical interpretation is a merely external one, in the sense that the analysis may "guide the development" of the performance, or the performance may "trigger" a critical analysis, or performance and analysis may "originate in

Fig. 4.1

tandem."[7] In opposition to Levinson, I want to say that an analysis or critical view may be part of a performance, either in the sense that it informs what is done by the performers or in the sense that it is part of what they project.

There exists a critical interpretation of the second movement of Beethoven's *Fourth Piano Concerto* according to which the movement symbolizes "the power of inner contemplation in overcoming aggression. . . . That aggressive opening phrase from the orchestra is neither commented upon nor contested. It is quite simply disregarded. In a rapt contemplation that verges towards mysticism the pianist conjures . . . magical chords from the keyboard."[8] (See figure 4.1.)

Levinson thinks that no imaginable performative interpretation could "include or imply" this critical interpretation, "even though, we have allowed, it comports well enough with it, and perhaps even gives some reason to believe that the performers, in their guise as critics or analysts, may hold something to that effect."[9]

It's hard to agree with him: playing can be aggressive, and contemplative, so if the orchestra chooses to play aggressively and the soloist contemplatively, aren't they executing this critical interpretation? Surely the performers can make these choices; the orchestral statements do not have to be done aggressively (but could express tragic power), and the piano's interjections can express grief and despair rather than contemplation.[10] Certainly the performers could have this critical view of the movement and they could intend to project it in their performance. Is Levinson suggesting that in some mysterious way their intention could not be achieved?

Contrast yet another critical interpretation: "its gruff string recitatives and cantabile solo phrases testing the power of poetry to tame harsh reality."[11] *This* critical interpretation, perhaps, cannot be projected by a performance of the movement, because the strings' representing reality and piano's representing poetry is not something that can be heard in the music.

Or consider an interpretation of the movement as alluding to the exchange between Orfeo and the Chorus in Gluck's *Orfeo*, act 2, scene 1, where Orfeo's pleas gradually subdue the Chorus, softening their implacable fury.[12] They are moved by his languishing for his lost love and by his description of his inner torment:

ORFEO: Ho con me l'inferno mio,
Me lo sento in mezzo al cor.
(ORFEO: I have my private hell;
I feel it in my heart.)

Orfeo has become the solo pianist, the Chorus has become the orchestra, and what the movement signifies is the lover's arousing of pity in the terrible forces of the underworld by his desolate song. Could performers intend to project this interpretation in performance? No, not without supplying the audience with the necessary codes. Merely to have these thoughts while performing the music would not be sufficient to produce such an intention.

Levinson's thesis, that no critical or analytical interpretation is projectable in performance, is subjected by him to a qualification. He wants to maintain it only for what he calls "robust" interpretations. His choice of examples suggests that by robust interpretations he means critical rather than analytical interpretations. But the Beethoven example stands against what he says: there the expressive qualities of aggression and contemplation form part of a critical rather than an analytical interpretation.

There is indeed a class of critical or analytical interpretations that are incapable of performative projection. Examples are narrative analyses such as Jan Kleczynski's,[13] according to which the ending of Chopin's *Third Ballade* "vividly depicts the ultimate drowning in some abyss, of the fated youth"; given an audience that had not antecedently heard this verbal analysis, a pianist could never hope, and therefore could never intend, to project the end of the ballade as depicting precisely this abysmal fate. Or again there are analyses that refer to formal features that cannot be heard. The general point is that some things can be heard in the music and some cannot; we must refer to the listener's experience of the music. This requirement of audibility can be weakened so that it demands merely audibility in a given context, which may include linguistic programs or clues; but the point will remain that what can't be heard in the music, even given these linguistic aids, can't be projected in performance.

Levinson's characterization of the class of critical or analytical interpretations that are not performatively projectable is not satisfactory; those interpretations are better characterized as ones that cannot be heard in the music.

Levinson presents several arguments in favor of his view, drawing attention to types of performance from which it would be impossible to infer a single critical or analytical interpretation of the music being performed. I shall consider two of these, neither of which I find satisfactory. The first argument concerns chamber music: "In chamber music there may be a single [performative interpretation] while the individual musicians have different [critical or analytical interpretations]."[14]

What does this mean? Does it mean that while the individual players' private views about the piece's meaning diverge, all consent to project a single view of the work in performance? Or does it mean that the performance projects no one's view of the piece (because all such views are, for example, too hopelessly poetic to be capable of embodiment in performance)? In either case, what is supposed to follow? In the first case, there *is* a single critical or analytical interpretation projected in performance, and other critical or analytical interpretations privately held by individual performers are in principle capable of such projection. In the second case, the players' critical or analytical interpretations are incapable of adequate performative projection. All we need conclude is (1) that there is a distinction between performers' privately held critical or analytical interpretations and those that they choose to project in performance, (2) that some critical or analytical interpretations are capable of adequate performative projection, and (3) that some are not.

Another of Levinson's arguments concerns the distinction between knowing how and knowing that "a performer does not need to be able to articulate reasons why his way of playing is right or true to the work's expressiveness or structure in order for us to say he possesses a [performative interpretation]."[15]

True. Nor—and this is more to the point—need performers be able to say what they did (knowing how doesn't imply knowing that). But what is shown by this? If by "having a performative interpretation" we mean that the performance projects an interpretation of the music, then to suppose that the performer has a performative interpretation of the music is to suppose that the performer projects either a critical or an analytical view of the music (since presumably interpretation involves either criticism or analysis). But then, all that Levinson's argument shows is the truism that there are cases in which the performer may be projecting a critical or analytical view of the work without being able to articulate that view in words. Just as a spider's web can have complex mathematical properties without the spider being able to say what they are, a performance can have a complex analysis that the performer is unable to articulate.

Peter Kivy has a different view of the relation between performative and critical interpretation:

> If we compare performing a piano sonata with what I take to be the paradigmatic instance of interpretation, namely, interpreting a literary work, we can, I think, plausibly characterize the latter as "telling how things go" and the former as "showing how things go". And in that both (to choose a neutral word) "*inform* us how things go", both can be thought of as interpreting.[16]

Kivy resists the idea (favored by philosophers such as Levinson) that such embodiments cannot be described *as* interpretations but merely *embody* them. The interpretation itself, according to these philosophers, is more abstract and intellectual than the performance: the same interpretation can occur in several performances and is something to be found at the level of conception, not the level of execution.[17] The opposing view (which I favor) holds that Madonna's performance of "Fever" *is* an interpretation. Its embodiment in her performance is essential to it. Any abstract description of it would falsify it by omitting some embodied detail.

Kivy is right: telling how something goes is not the same as showing how it goes. He is also right in saying that the term "interpretation" can be applied in both cases. Both cases involve the representation of an object and its subsequent subsumption under a significance-endowing concept.

Performative interpretation is, then, interpretation, and it is distinguished from other kinds of interpretation by its object and its mode of representation.

Because performative interpretation is conceptual as well as practical—where this conceiving is done (and projected) by the performers—it does not present itself transparently to its audience. The very identification of a performative interpretation by those who are not engaged in it is itself a matter of interpretation. Performative interpretation is always *imputed*. The nontransparency of performative interpretation to its audience is well captured in a remark by Ates Orga and Nikolai Demidenko: "The romantic piano masters of the past—Pachmann, Rachmaninov, Busoni, Hofmann, Paderewski at his best, Friedman, Horowitz—all had a secret: from their playing, it could never be said with certainty whether or not they were being serious or teasing."[18]

CLASSIFICATION BY OBJECT AND GOVERNING CONCEPT

Some kinds of interpretation have a characteristic sort of object and a characteristic sort of governing concept. Let's focus on one such kind—critical interpretation, with its characteristic objects (artworks) and its characteristic array of governing concepts drawn from various critical discourses.

The distinguishing mark of critical interpretations does not reside solely in the fact that they have artworks for their objects. Artworks are also subject to performative and scientific interpretation. What distinguishes critical interpretation, in addition to its characteristic objects, is the array of governing concepts it employs—concepts of artistic genre, artistic purpose, and tradition, among others.

Critical interpretations employ various types of significance-systems. The way these systems work is by assigning particular significances to particular items, or types of significance to types of items. But they don't do this neat; they assign significance only relative to certain (perhaps vaguely stated) background conditions such as facts about the artist's oeuvre, the artist's life, theories of artistic worth or artistic production, theories of interpretation. Via these systems and background conditions, the object gets to be seen as instantiating some governing concept—

it is seen as *representing* something, or *expressing* something, or *being about* something, or *being a response to* something, or *belonging in a certain tradition*, or *exhibiting certain formal features*, etc. To see the work in these various ways is, variously, to make sense of it.

Albert Lubin makes sense of Van Gogh's painting *The Potato Eaters* by interpreting it as an expression of mourning for the artist's dead brother. How does he do this? He highlights the direction and expressive content of the subjects' gazes, the wall separating the older woman and man, the name "Vincent" on the chair at the left, the lantern, the steam rising from the hot potatoes and coffee, and (crucially) the child in the foreground.[19] This is his interpretive representation of the painting. Lubin then appeals to background information consisting of biographical details (the artist's preoccupation with lights in the sky, the birth and death of his brother—also called Vincent—a year before the artist's birth), and a preliminary sketch for the painting containing only the three figures highlighted in Lubin's representation. Given this background, and given a significance-system that includes ways of connecting information about the artist's life and oeuvre with the representational character of the artist's works, the painting is interpretable as a representation of mourning. Lubin captures it: "It would seem that Vincent was portraying the grieving mother who could not mother him; her spirit remained with the dead but perfect child who stood between them, separating them in the painting as in life."[20]

CLASSIFICATION BY OBJECT, REPRESENTATION, AND GOVERNING CONCEPT

Some kinds of interpretation are characterized by a combination of type of object, type of representation, and type of governing concept. I shall mention four—arrangement, variation, parody, and explanation.

Arrangement

Peter Kivy makes much of the notion of a musical arrangement and of its similarity to that of a performance.[21] His argument is that since both arrangements of a work and performances of it are called "versions" of the work, and since a version is an interpretation, performances are like arrangements in that they are creative as well as being interpretive.[22] He concludes that arrangements are interpretations because they are versions, versions being interpretations:

> For the arranger, unlike the composer, cannot start from scratch. He or she starts with a preexistent work, of which a version must be contrived; and in order for his or her result to be a version of the work and not a new work in its own right it must be, whatever else it is, a possible, plausible way that work goes. Thus the arranger must have an idea of how the work goes in order to make a credible version of it. He or she must, in other words, have an interpretation, be an interpreter.[23]

The argument is flawed. Penitents must first of all be sinners, but that is not to say that repentance is a sin. Similarly, if arrangers must first of all be interpreters, that isn't to say that arrangements are interpretations. Nonetheless, I agree with Kivy that arrangements are interpretations, depending as they do on instrumentation and style. The notion of a musical arrangement is the notion of an interpretation with characteristic types of objects, representation, and significance. A musical work is represented in a new medium or style and is thereby transformed into something bearing the type of significance that belongs to that medium or style. The transformation may endow the work with heightened spirituality (as with Bach's chorale transcriptions), or it may vulgarize the work (as with Stokowski's arrangements of Bach); it may turn one musical genre (mellifluous song) into another (dazzling pianism), or it may reduce a complex work to a form manageable by amateurs. There is no end to the changes that can be rung on musical significance.

CHAPTER FOUR

Variation and Parody

Nelson Goodman claims that "variations upon a work, whether in the same or a different medium, and still more, sets of variations—are interpretations of the work."[24] This seems right. Variations are *of* musical (or pictorial) works; they represent those works in characteristic ways; and they carry the special type of significance that is imported by the musical term "variation." Goodman himself mentions some of the methods by which variations get derived from themes: deletion, supplementation, deformation, reordering, and reweighting.[25] These are—in my terms—modes of representation.

Variation and arrangement are distinct kinds of interpretation; variation, unlike arrangement, need not change the medium or the style of the original. Nonetheless, variation and arrangement can occur in the same work—as in Beethoven's variations on arias from *The Magic Flute* arranged for cello and piano.

Goodman notes the similarities between parodies and variations, while recognizing that "the point of a parody is quite different from that of the usual variation."[26] Certainly as traditionally understood, a parody ridicules its object—something that variations generally do not do. But Goodman is right, I believe, in his implied statement that parody is a form of interpretation.

Like all interpretation, parody attributes a type of significance to its object. This significance not only differs from what the author might have intended but actually undermines that intended significance. The parodist attributes a perverted sense to the object, and to do so must represent the object in particular ways. Techniques of parodic representation (in this traditional sense) include distortion and assimilation to alien contexts.

Linda Hutcheson makes use of a different—and peculiarly twentieth-century—notion of parody, as a "process of revising, replaying, inverting, and 'trans-contextualizing' previous works of art."[27]

Herbert Lindenberger points out that parody in this sense need not ridicule its object.[28] Despite this difference, it seems clear that this type of parody is also a form of interpretation, as Lindenberger writes (referring to some recent operatic productions):

> Chéreau's, Sellars's, and their various colleagues' interpretations are precisely that—interpretations. However much they may try to shock the opera-going public, they also seek, in a serious and sustained manner, to make contemporary sense out of an older text. . . . [P]arody, even in this postmodern usage, implies some sort of interpretative gesture on the part of author or audience.[29]

Explanation

Let's return to Lavoisier's oxygen theory. Lavoisier portrays his own thought as structured by the chief difficulties of chemistry (they constitute the object of interpretation); a way of conceptualizing them (this is the manner of representing the object); a theory expressible in those concepts and applying to the said difficulties (this is the significance-system); and, ensuing from that application, an explanation of the initial difficulties (the governing concept is "explained by the oxygen theory").

In general, a scientific interpretation of a natural phenomenon aims to make sense of it by finding a way of representing it that can be integrated into a body of explanatory theory. Thus scientific explanations are distinguished from other interpretations in their objects (nature), in their modes of representation, and in their type of significance (explanation). In particular, explanations operate with a characteristic type of significance-system that links representations of natural phenomena with their explanations by means of *natural laws*. Not every interpretation operates with this particular type of significance-system, and for this reason it is clear that not all interpretation is explanation. Thus the answer to our sixth question (What is the relation between interpretation and explanation?) is that while explanation is a form of interpretation, not all interpretation takes this form.

Explanations by intentional causes are a species of explanatory interpretation. When I interpret the look on your face as a friendly smile, I make sense of your look by supposing that it is explained by the existence of an intention to acknowledge my presence in a friendly way. The object of my interpretation is your smile, which I represent as an effect of a yet-to-be-determined mental cause; and relying on folk psychological theory as a significance-system, I subsume it under the concept "explained by an intention to signal friendship." The significance of this subsumption is that it gives me a causal understanding of your smile.

In general, an explanation of a particular interpretive object aims at understanding that object. But not all interpretation shares this aim. Many constructive interpretations are content to amplify on their objects in ways that construct significant wholes incorporating those objects rather than aiming at an exposition of the object's already-existing significance. And transgressive parodic interpretations may even aim at *misunderstanding* their objects. There is the answer to our fifth question (What is the relation between interpretation and understanding?).

NOTES

1. E. D. Hirsch Jr., *The Aims of Interpretation* (Chicago: University of Chicago Press, 1976), 19.
2. Hirsch's is a narrower sense of the word "significance" than mine.
3. Hirsch, *Aims*, 2–3.
4. Hans-Georg Gadamer, *Truth and Method*, trans. Joel Weinsheimer and Donald G. Marshall, 2d ed. (New York: Continuum, 1994), 397.
5. Jerrold Levinson, "Performative versus Critical Interpretation in Music," in *The Interpretation of Music: Philosophical Essays*, ed. Michael Krausz (Oxford: Clarendon Press, 1993) 33–60, 33.
6. Levinson, "Performative versus Critical Interpretation," 36–37.
7. Levinson, "Performative versus Critical Interpretation," 36–37.
8. Antony Hopkins, *Understanding Music* (London: J. M. Dent, 1979), 135–40.
9. Levinson, "Performative versus Critical Interpretation," 40–41.

10. Cf. Charles Rosen, *The Classical Style* (London: Faber & Faber, 1971), 211.

11. Douglas Johnson, liner notes to Beethoven, *Piano Concertos Nos. 3 & 4*, Melvyn Tan and the London Classical Players, Roger Norrington, EMI, CDC 7 49815 2, 1989.

12. Such an allusion is suggested by Johnson, liner notes to Beethoven, *Piano Concertos*.

13. *Chopin's Greater Works*, trans Natalie Janota (London, 1896), 68.

14. Levinson, "Performative versus Critical Interpretation," 44.

15. Levinson, "Performative versus Critical Interpretation," 47.

16. Peter Kivy, *Authenticities: Philosophical Reflections on Musical Performance* (Ithaca, N.Y.: Cornell University Press, 1995), 137.

17. See, e.g., Michael Krausz, *Rightness and Reasons: Interpretation in Cultural Practices* (Ithaca, N.Y.: Cornell University Press, 1993), 18 ff.

18. Ates Orga and Nikolai Demidenko, liner notes to Chopin, *The Four Scherzi*, Nikolai Demidenko, Hyperion CDA66514, 1991.

19. Krausz, *Rightness and Reasons*, 73–74.

20. Albert Lubin, *Stranger on the Earth: A Psychological Biography of Vincent Van Gogh* (New York: Holt, Reinhart & Winston, 1972), 100.

21. Kivy, *Authenticities*, 133–38.

22. Kivy emphasizes the analogies between performances and arrangements: in addition to the similarities already mentioned, he notes that both performances and arrangements fall under the kind of interpretation that "shows how things go" rather than "telling how things go." So it may be timely to remember that there is a fundamental difference between performances and arrangements in that only the latter are works.

23. Kivy, *Authenticities*, 137.

24. Nelson Goodman, "Variations on Variation—Or Picasso Back to Bach," in *Reconceptions in Philosophy and Other Arts and Sciences*, Nelson Goodman and Catherine Z. Elgin (London: Routledge, 1988), 66–82, 82.

25. Goodman, "Variations," 67.

26. Goodman, "Variations," 73.

27. Linda Hutcheson, *A Theory of Parody: The Teachings of Twentieth-Century Art Forms* (New York: Methuen, 1985), 11.

28. Herbert Lindenberger, *Opera in History from Monteverdi to Cage* (Stanford, Calif.: Stanford University Press, 1998), 241.

29. Lindenberger, *Opera in History*, 259.

5

GENERAL RULES

The Uninspired Archaeologist and Freud's *Macbeth*

Using the model outlined in chapter 2, we can say just what a particular interpretation's elements are. But having identified an interpretation, how do we judge it? Are all interpretations equally good? Is there truth in interpretation? Of some interpretations we say that they are brilliant or insightful, routine or unilluminating; what justifies us in preferring one interpretation over another in these ways? These are the issues collected under our seventh question for a theory of interpretation (How are interpretations evaluated?).

In this chapter we'll see that there are a number of general rules by which every interpretation must be judged. Beyond that, each interpretation must be judged against its own specific aims. Let's begin, however, by noting the aims that any operation of interpretation must have.

AIMS OF INTERPRETATION

Our model defines interpretation as aiming to endow a given object with a particular type of significance by subsuming a representation of it under a governing concept. Clearly, therefore, interpretations must be evaluated by reference to their success in achieving this broad aim. An interpretation's success depends on two factors. First, the governing concept must endow the object with *significance*. Second, the governing concept must give a *comprehensive* coverage of the object. Recall the qualities that Lavoisier prized in his oxygen theory: significance (the "dissipation of difficulties," "a single principle," and "astonishing simplicity") and comprehensiveness ("all the phenomena").

Significance

Interpretation aims to endow its object with significance. One way of seeing this is to consider something that looks like interpretation in other ways but does not aim at endowing significance. An example is perhaps provided by John Cage's *Europeras 1 & 2*—a work whose action has been summarized as follows:[1]

> Each singer was asked to choose a group of arias that could be completed in no more than thirty and no less than twenty minutes. Several renditions took place at once.... Although the orchestral accompaniments were drawn largely from the list of operas whose arias the singers were presenting, only fragments of accompaniments (and these are in no way tied to the arias as they are being sung), all chosen by means of chance operations, were actually performed.[2]

Critics are divided on whether this work makes a significant comment on the operatic material it recycles.[3] On one view, the work makes a significant, and supposedly final, statement lampooning the whole operatic art form. If that view is accepted, the work should be seen as an interpretation of the tradition of operatic performances and works. On another view, the work simply does not present any unified governing concept and cannot therefore be seen as offering an interpretation of anything at all.

What has the superficial appearance of a governing concept might not have the capacity to endow significance: it might be bland, flat, or noncommittal. Clearly, an interpretation might fail in this way even if it represents its object comprehensively. Imagine an uninspired archaeologist who meticulously labels all her samples "A," "B," "C," and so on, but who is unable to attach any significance to the samples. She cannot make any progress by saying "Well, all the samples fall under label 'A' or label 'B,' etc." This description doesn't express a mode of significance.

In order to express a mode of significance, a governing concept must be unitary. This is not to say that it needs to be expressible in a single word; it is to say that it should possess a conceptual, rather than a verbal, unity. (The uninspired archaeologist failed to achieve such a unity.) Unity, in turn, implies simplicity. As Paul Thagard notes, "Scientists tend to be skeptical of hypotheses that require myriad ad hoc assumptions in their explanations. There is nothing wrong in principle in having explanations that draw on many assumptions, but we should prefer theories that generate explanations using a unified core of hypotheses."[4] The same applies to interpretation in general.

The uninspired archaeologist may have a number of concepts that severally apply to distinct subsets of her examples, but what she doesn't have is a single overarching concept that draws all those individual concepts together in a coherent whole. Similarly, Cage's *Europeras* goes to some lengths to block the projection of any unifying concept that imposes a coherence on its disparate elements. In both these cases, failure to endow the object with significance is accompanied by failure to make the parts of the object cohere. By contrast, in our earlier examples, success in endowing the object with significance was accompanied by success in imposing a coherence on its parts. In recognizing the prompter's utterance, the audience also recognized a sequence of sounds that cohered in a particular way; Lavoisier's oxygen theory, in making sense of the phenomena of combustion, gave those phenomena a coherence among themselves and displayed them as cohering with a wider set of phenomena. So we are led to ask whether, whenever the object of interpretation has parts, success in endowing it with significance *implies* success in making its parts cohere.

CHAPTER FIVE

Before considering the question directly, I shall try to deflect some considerations that suggest a negative answer.

One line of reasoning that suggests a negative answer goes like this: critical sense can be made about an object precisely by showing the object to be incoherent, so the making of sense can't imply the attribution of coherence.

True, Umberto Eco seems to think that we can make sense of a text only by attributing coherence to it: "Any interpretation of a certain portion of a text can be accepted if it is confirmed and must be rejected if it is challenged by another portion of the same text. In this sense the internal textual coherence controls the otherwise uncontrollable drives of the reader."[5]

But there is an unwarranted slide here from the idea that an interpretation should itself be coherent to the idea that it should impute coherence to its object. Eco forgets, perhaps, that not all interpretation attempts to make its object make sense; sometimes it is a matter rather of making sense *about* the object. But in that case, couldn't one make sense about an object precisely by showing how, and why, the object doesn't make sense—by showing the object to be *incoherent*? It seems so if, for instance, we consider Michael Tanner's critical comments about Wagner's *Ring*:

> Since he was among the greatest composers, more interested in the symphonic than the operatic tradition which he inherited, the Ring's musical structure was bound to be, in various ways, at odds with its dramatic content, seeming to give the latter a coherence which in its honesty it can't possess. The resulting dislocations are among the chief reasons for the work's perennial appeal. A promise of wholeness is held out by one part of it, and denied by another. It is difficult to envisage a time when we shall no longer want to explore the conflicts within it, for that would suggest that we no longer had them in ourselves.[6]

Tanner imputes a kind of incoherence to the *Ring*. In doing so, he implies that a certain kind of sense cannot be made of it; we should give up trying to make it, as a whole, make sense. The music doesn't cohere, to a sufficiently convincing degree, with the drama. At the same time Tanner himself makes good sense in writing about the *Ring*, and in doing so, his thoughts possess a convincing logical coherence.

But more than that. While Tanner denies a certain kind of coherence to the *Ring*, he finds another kind of coherence there. Suppose (he seems to say) you wanted to devise a work that modeled the conflicts that we experience in our own lives, conflicts and dislocations generated by promises of wholeness offered by one part of our lives and denied by other parts—then (if you had the talent) you might well come up with something like the *Ring*.

And this brings us back to the main point. If it can be held that Tanner's account does indeed attribute a kind of coherence to the *Ring*, then his account doesn't refute our hypothesis that to attribute significance is *eo ipso* to attribute coherence. On the other hand, if it stretches credulity to say that in talking of dislocations and conflicts within a work, we are attributing a kind of coherence to it, then we should abandon our hypothesis. We'll come back to this.

Another argument for driving a wedge between significance and coherence goes like this: Sense can be made of an object in a nontraditional way, and when this happens, the interpretation doesn't cohere with the tradition of interpreting the object.

Eco (again) thinks that an interpretation can be successful only if it coheres with the tradition of interpretations of the given object: "Certain interpretations can be recognized as unsuccessful because they are like a mule, that is, they are unable to produce new interpretations or cannot be confronted with the traditions of the previous interpretations."[7]

But it's one thing to demand that individual interpretations be internally coherent and another to demand that sets of interpretations of the same object cohere in traditions. There is no reason in general why a given interpretation should cohere with the object's traditional interpretations. The modern Wagnerian productions that Tanner finds so objectionable make little use of traditional interpretations. However, there is a ready reply to this objection.

Nontraditional interpretations don't attempt to interpret the tradition but the work (the *Ring*, for example), so it isn't relevant to point out that they don't succeed in presenting a coherent view of the tradition when they aim simply to present a coherent view of the work.

Here is a third way of trying to prise significance and coherence apart. If coherence implies truth, then interpreters could find significance where they don't find coherence—for example, in works of fiction.

But coherence doesn't imply truth. Not even logical coherence implies truth, since a logically coherent set may include falsehoods. In addition, not all coherence is logical: elements in a musical or pictorial structure can be coherent or incoherent.

So far we haven't found a reason for rejecting the hypothesis that significance implies coherence. Let's try again, this time by asking, What is coherence? Laurence Bonjour takes coherence to be primarily a relation between two elements and only secondarily a feature of systems of elements.[8] Bonjour states five principles governing coherence:

> (1) A system of beliefs is coherent only if it is logically consistent.
> (2) A system of beliefs is coherent in proportion to its degree of probabilistic consistency.
> (3) The coherence of a system of beliefs is increased by the presence of inferential connections between its component beliefs and increased in proportion to the number and strength of such connections.
> (4) The coherence of a system of beliefs is diminished to the extent to which it is divided into subsystems of beliefs which are relatively unconnected to each other by inferential connections.
> (5) The coherence of a system of beliefs is decreased in proportion to the presence of unexplained anomalies in the believed content of the system.[9]

Alvin Plantinga questions the first of these, proposing instead of logical consistency "something like absence of *obvious* impossibility, or perhaps impossibility that *would* be obvious after a certain period of reflection."[10] Plantinga also questions the second principle, pointing out that "what is improbable is surely the rule rather than the exception. That precisely *that* mosquito should bite you precisely when and where it does, . . .—either these things are all improbable in the relevant sense or else I have no idea what the relevant sense is."[11]

Bonjour's notion of coherence requires that there is a threshold of coherence below which a system of beliefs is simply incoherent, and above which coherence is a matter of degree. Plantinga's first query brings out one problem with such a notion. *Proof* of coherence must, for Bonjour, depend on a consistency-proof for the body of beliefs in question. This is counterintuitive in the case of formal deductive systems, to which one would want to attribute a certain degree of coherence even in advance of a formal consistency-proof.

Plantinga's second query brings out a different problem for Bonjour's notion of coherence. It seems that, for Bonjour, no system incorporating the belief that "precisely *that* mosquito should bite you precisely when and where it does" can possess a high degree of coherence. Plantinga takes it for granted that this result is absurd. It does indeed seem so, if we think that the proposition that the mosquito bit me coheres with the proposition that the mosquito was in my vicinity at the time.

Assuming, then, that Bonjour's first two principles should be dropped, we are left with a notion of coherence as the degree of connectivity of beliefs in a system with respect to a relation of logical implication, that is, the degree to which any two beliefs in the system are linked by a path, each step of which is either the relation of logical implication or its converse. According to this notion, every axiomatic deductive system is 100 percent coherent, whether or not it is logically consistent.

According to this notion, coherence belongs to the *system*, not to the pairs of elements within the system; but coherence is *realized* through relations among those elements.

Such a notion can be generalized: a domain is coherent with

respect to a given relation to the extent that the relation is connected in that domain. The coherence-relation needn't be logical implication. It could be a relation of narrative, pictorial, or musical coherence. Because of this, the generalized notion of coherence is useful for the theory of interpretation. Interpretations will be coherent to different degrees, relative to different coherence-relations.

If the domain partitions into two fully coherent domains that can't be linked to each other by any product of the coherence-relation and its converse, then the domain as a whole is not fully coherent. Indeed, if the domain contains two elements that can't be linked by any product of the relation and its converse, then it is less than 100 percent coherent. The domain's degree of coherence with respect to a given relation is simply the logical probability of any two elements' being linked by a path, each step of which is either the relation or its converse.

The question whether in attributing significance to an object we thereby attribute a degree of coherence to it, then, comes down to this: In attributing significance to the object, do we state or show a degree of connectedness among the object's parts with respect to some relation? The question should be restricted to *global* interpretations, since these are the only ones where the object, as an object of that interpretation, has parts. And the answer is yes. Consider the interpretation of *The Magic Flute* as a transformation opera. The interpretation goes like this: The work's parts are its scenes, and a high proportion of these involve elements of transformation. So the parts are to a high degree connected as parts with transformational aspects. We find a significance in the work precisely to the extent that we find this type of connectedness among its parts.

A similar analysis can be applied to other global interpretations—for example, to Lavoisier's global interpretation of the phenomena of combustion and calcification, to performative interpretations of musical or dramatic works, and to any global interpretation that is realized through cognate interpretations of the object's parts.

Interpretations that assign representational significance to an object are of this type. In interpreting an object as representing a face, we interpret one of its parts as representing the eyes, another the mouth, and so on. So significance also implies coherence in representational interpretations. And it seems that in general in attributing significance to a global object of interpretation, we thereby attribute coherence to various local objects. Consequently, significance is a matter of degree, just as coherence is.

In the light of this analysis of coherence, we can now see that Tanner's interpretation of the *Ring* is indeed coherent. Its global view of the work is realized in a set of cognate views of the work's parts. These parts are seen as possessing a kind of connectedness, namely, through relations of conflict and dislocation, and these conflictual concepts govern Tanner's global view of the work. To present a work in such terms is indeed to attach a type of significance to it, though not the kind of significance one would attach to an ultimately successful music-drama.

Comprehensiveness

Interpretation aims at comprehensive coverage of its object. An activity that might be like interpretation in other ways would not deserve the name "interpretation" if it did not have this aim. It might, for example, be better termed "plundering" or "ransacking."

There are two junctures in the operation of interpretation at which the issue of comprehensiveness comes up: in the relation of the object-as-represented to the object, and in the relation of the governing concept to the object-as-represented. An interpretation can be comprehensive or noncomprehensive, either in its representation of the object or in its conceptualization of the object-as-represented. Sometimes interpreters don't succeed in representing all that should be represented in the object; and sometimes they don't succeed in comprehensively conceiving of the object-as-represented: the conception seems forced or the object-as-represented resists this type of conceptualization.

A note of warning: The requirement that interpretive representation be comprehensive should not be taken to rule out selectivity in interpretive representation. Such representation may very well be selective. What matters is whether the features it selects are fully representative of the object for the interpretive purposes in hand.

William Whewell uses the term "consilience" for a particular type of interpretive breadth. He explains:

> I have spoken . . . of the *Consilience of Inductions*, as one of the *Tests of Hypotheses*, and have exemplified it in many instances; for example, the theory of universal gravitation, obtained by induction from the motions of the planets, was found to explain also that peculiar motion of the spheroidal earth which produces the Precession of the Equinoxes. . . . I may compare such occurrences to a case of interpreting an unknown character, in which two different inscriptions, deciphered by different persons, should have given the same alphabet.[12]

What consilience amounts to, it seems, is that a hypothesis (or more generally an interpretation) is found to provide comprehensive coverage not only of the initial object of interpretation but of a range of other objects as well. Such a consilience shows that the hypothesis explains more than it was originally proposed as explaining. And this in turn suggests that the initial object of interpretation can be taken as a fragment of a wider global object that admits of the same general interpretation—somewhat as we found in chapter 2 that the use of the concept "transformation" in interpreting the *Flugwerk* scene in *The Magic Flute* allows us to treat that scene as a fragment that can be interpretively integrated into the whole opera. In both cases the initial object is reconceived as a local object in some wider interpretive context. It is significant that in both these cases we have good reason to expect that there will be such a wider context. The motions of the planets can be expected to be part of some wider system of physical laws; and scene 16 can be expected to have stylistic links with other parts of the opera. In the absence of such expectations, consilience would have to be regarded as mere coincidence.

Sigmund Freud proposed an interpretation of Lady Macbeth as barren—an interpretation based on her "unsex me now" line. Freud thought that it would be poetic justice

> if Lady Macbeth had suffered the unsexing she had demanded of the spirits of murder. I believe one could without more ado explain the illness of Lady Macbeth, the transformation of her callousness into penitence, as a reaction to her childlessness, by which she is convinced of her impotence against the decrees of nature, and at the same time admonished that she has only herself to blame if her crime has been barren of the better part of its results.[13]

Opposing this interpretation, Harold Bloom asks:

> Why then does she say that she has given suck? As the wife of a powerful thane who is the king's cousin, she is too highly placed to have nursed any child but her own. We must conclude that there was at least one child, but it died. Nor can she have been left barren; Macbeth in praise of her resolution urges her to bring forth men-children only.[14]

The dispute is about the comprehensiveness of the two interpretations. Bloom's own representation of Lady Macbeth includes passages in the play that Freud's representation passes over. He can argue that Freud's is an unsuitable representation for interpreting Lady Macbeth as barren because it is too selective. It passes over some features of the object that are relevant to this interpretation—relevant because they conflict with it.

GENERAL CONSTRAINTS ON INTERPRETATION

Because interpretation has the aims it does, its terms are constrained.

CHAPTER FIVE

Constraints on the Object

Anything at all can be an object of interpretation to the extent that someone might want to make sense of anything at all. At the same time, an interpretation's object might be poorly chosen, in the sense that it is itself the outcome of a poor piece of interpreting—for example a badly edited text. In this case the interpreter could have chosen a better object. So should we say that one constraint on the object is that it be well chosen? Not for this reason. Strictly speaking, the interpretation of an object shouldn't be condemned on this account. It is a distinct act of interpreting and should be judged only relative to its object. The poorly chosen object is a poor interpretation of some further object, and it is *that* interpretation that flouts some interpretive constraint.

Consider now another case of an inappropriate object of interpretation—the "meteorological" phenomena of ancient astronomy. This class of phenomena (we want to say) is poorly chosen: it is simply not a proper object of interpretation. But didn't we say that *anything* can be an object of interpretation? The contradiction can be resolved if we recall the requirement of significance. This requirement implies that there must be a governing concept (and type of significance) such that the object falls under that concept if any interpretation of that object is to succeed. This is the constraint of *appropriateness of the object,* and it is relativized to a particular governing concept and type of significance.

The "meteorological" (in the ancient sense) is not an appropriate object *relative to natural explanation* as a type of significance. It may be appropriate relative to another type of significance. Thus there is a constraint on objects of interpretation that they be appropriate to the governing concept and type of significance being employed in the current operation of interpreting.

In short, while there are no limits on what we might want to make sense of, there are limits on what we can succeed in making sense of, relative to a given significance-system.

Constraints on the Representation

What constrains the kind of representation used in an interpretive operation? The representation should be an appropriate one through which to adapt the object to the interpretation's governing concept. What is appropriate depends both on the object and on the governing concept. The requirement of *comprehensiveness* implies that the representation should be suitable. In order for a representation to be suitable, it must pick up all those features of the object that are relevant to the governing concept's application to the object. The representation must, so to speak, preserve significance, in the sense that if the chosen type of significance belongs to the object-as-represented, then it belongs to the object. This specification should be contrasted with Margolis's comparatively vague requirement that an acceptable interpretation not conflict with minimal describable properties of the object.[15] Our idea of a suitable representation is an attempt to say just what should be included among the object's "minimal describable properties."

Consistent with this constraint, the object may be treated selectively. Notice, however, that selectivity and cuts always need justifying. In the absence of such justifications, interpretations can be criticized for leaving some aspect of the object out of account.

Another way in which a representation could be inappropriate is if it is in the wrong mode (relative as always to the governing concept and type of significance). Suppose Daniel *sings* the words on the wall when asked for an explanation of them. He has represented the object but not in the way required by a governing concept of explanation. To represent in song is not (of itself) to explain. Thus there is a constraint of *appropriateness of the representation*, relativized to the governing concept and type of significance.

Constraints on the Governing Concept

Given the aims of interpretation, the governing concept should be *comprehensive* and *significance endowing* (relative to the object-as-represented). This implies that it should be unitary. For the interpretation to be unitary, the concept must really be *a concept* and not (as Aristotle would say) a mere heap. For it to be comprehensive, the object-as-represented (including both the content and the manner of representation) must fit the governing concept. For it to be significance endowing, the governing concept must express a mode of significance, or in Margolis's words it must express "admissible myths or schemes of imagination."[16]

RULES OF INTERPRETATION

We can sum up our discussion of success in interpretation under three rules:

1. The governing concept expresses a mode of interpretation, that is, it has the capacity to be significance-endowing.

2. The governing concept actually endows the object-as-represented comprehensively with significance and consequently with coherence.

3. The representation is a suitable one, in the sense that it preserves significance; that is, if the governing concept applies to the object-as-represented, then it applies to the object.

These rules, though independent of one another in principle, sometimes interact in practice. Recall Michael Tanner's discussion of the Bayreuth production of Wagner's *Ring* that concluded with a nuclear holocaust.[17] It seems that in this production the director's interpretation of the work was not a comprehensive one because it failed to attend sufficiently to the music. If one considers the whole production as a collaborative interpretation of the work, then it too seems to have been flawed in a different, but connected, way. It did not present a coherent view of the work; but even though coherence is in principle distinct from comprehensiveness, the incoherence of this interpretation was a consequence of the fact that the director's interpretation was not comprehensive. Finally, if one considers the members of the audience as interpreters, it's clear that the failings in the director's interpretation, and the interpretive incoherence of the production as a whole, debarred the spectators from attributing certain types of experiential significance to the production. Tanner's point is that an audience is denied the chance to form certain types of interpretation if they are denied the possibility of having certain types of experience.

The rules I have stated are general in the sense that they state conditions on what can be a successful *product* of interpretation. They are not intended to state conditions on the successful conduct of the *process* of interpreting. Therefore they are not intended to furnish a method of interpretation. Further, given the great variety of ways in which the protoprocess of interpretation can be executed, and given the great variety of practices that are encompassed under the rubric of interpretation, the quest for a method of interpretation seems to me to be a vain one. There is the answer to another of our initial questions.

NOTES

1. Discussed in Herbert Lindenberger, *Opera in History from Monteverdi to Cage* (Stanford, Calif.: Stanford University Press, 1998), chap. 8.
2. Lindenberger, *Opera in History*, 242–43.
3. Lindenberger, *Opera in History*, 241.
4. Paul Thagard, *Conceptual Revolutions* (Princeton, N.J.: Princeton University Press, 1992), 67.
5. Umberto Eco, *The Limits of Interpretation* (Bloomington: Indiana University Press, 1990), 59.

6. Michael Tanner, *Wagner* (London: Flamingo, 1997), 182–83.

7. Umberto Eco, "Reply," in *Interpretation and Overinterpretation*, ed. Stefan Collini (Cambridge: Cambridge University Press, 1992), 150.

8. Laurence Bonjour, *The Structure of Empirical Knowledge* (Cambridge: Harvard University Press, 1985).

9. Bonjour, *The Structure of Empirical Knowledge*, 95, 98–99.

10. Alvin Plantinga, *Warrant: The Current Debate* (New York: Oxford University Press, 1993), 91.

11. Plantinga, *Warrant*, 91.

12. W. Whewell, *Of Induction, with Especial Reference to Mr. J. Stuart Mill's System of Logic* (London: John W. Parker, 1849), 61.

13. Harold Bloom, *The Western Canon: The Books and School of the Ages* (London: Papermac, 1995), 388.

14. Bloom, *The Western Canon*, 388.

15. Joseph Margolis, *Art and Philosophy* (Brighton: Harvester, 1980), 159

16. Margolis, *Art and Philosophy*, 159.

17. See chapter 1, above.

6

SPECIAL RULES

THE OFFSTAGE PIANO AND ELVIS'S "HOUND DOG"

Any interpretation, if it is to be successful, has to make comprehensive sense of its object by representing it suitably. But success can amount to very different things in different cases. There are two principal causes of this diversity, and they derive from the different types of significance and the different ways in which an interpretive representation can be suitable for the task in hand.

TYPES OF SIGNIFICANCE

Three types of significance are especially prominent in interpretation. The first of these is the type of significance that is offered by natural explanations.

Natural Explanatory Significance

I don't pretend to give a comprehensive account of natural explanatory significance, but I will draw attention to two of its distinctive features. First, the significance-system on which such interpretations draw is a system of natural laws. The second distinctive feature of natural explanatory significance is one that

Paul Thagard calls "data priority." I shall discuss these in turn.

The significance-systems used by interpreters may include various imaginative elements—even whole fictional worlds. They need not be confined to a system of natural laws, even if fictional worlds invariably turn out to be tacitly based on the laws of nature as found in the actual world. What marks natural explanations off from other interpretations is their reliance on a significance-system made up *entirely* of laws of nature. To make sense of things by giving a natural explanation of them is to take Nature as a great system, an ultimate given, and to seek to refer things back in logical steps to this great system.

Thagard explains what he means by data priority: "In saying that a proposition describing the results of observation has a degree of acceptability on its own, I am not suggesting that it is indubitable, only that it can stand on its own more successfully than a hypothesis whose sole justification is what it explains."[1]

What this amounts to is the requirement that the explanation be fitted to the data rather than the other way around. Data priority is indeed a requirement for explanatory interpretations. However, it is not a requirement for constructive interpretations, where the direction of fit may be the reverse of what natural science demands.

These two features of natural explanation are independent of one another. You can have a significance-system made up solely of natural laws in the absence of data priority, for example, if you rig the evidence to suit your theory while respecting natural laws. And you can have data priority without a significance-system of natural laws—for example, in "authentic" performance where the significance-system is a corpus of surviving information about period performance style rather than the laws of nature.

Intentional Significance

Prominent among the species of significance assigned by interpreters is intentional significance, by which I mean significance as a product of intentional action. This type of significance doesn't exclude explanatory significance: we frequently want to explain something as possessing intentional significance. In such a case the natural laws to which we appeal will be laws of human nature.

To attribute intentional significance to an object is always to offer an explanation. But not all explanation seeks to endow its object with intentional significance; explanations of the nonhuman world that aim for this type of significance would standardly be deemed defective. The reason for their defectiveness is clear from our theory, on the assumption that there are in reality no natural laws entailing that nonhuman phenomena have significance as intentional, even if superstition might occasionally have it otherwise.

Two complementary principles guide many interpretations that assign intentional significance to their objects. These are the principle of charity and the fusion of horizons. The former is a principle constraining interpreters to maximize truth or rationality in the object of interpretation.[2] It is sometimes called the principle of humanity.[3] Here is an example of its operation.

The newsreader, following her script, announces that the maximum temperature in Canberra will be minus 18. She immediately adds, "That can't be right." What she means is not just that the forecast in her script can't be correct, but that it can't have been intended by the script's author. In making this correction, the newsreader is applying the principle of charity by assuming that the author of the script cannot have believed that the maximum temperature was going to be minus 18 and cannot have intended to promulgate such a forecast. The effect of the principle is thus to correct an attribution of a belief, and an intention, that conflicts with the presumption of a certain commonality in human beliefs and intentions.

The fusion of horizons, by contrast, is a principle that emphasizes the *specificities* of the human condition. It emphasizes human difference rather than human sameness. The set of assumptions available to any given person constitutes what Gadamer calls that person's *horizon*. "A hermeneutical situation is determined by the prejudices that we bring with us. They constitute, then, the horizon of a particular present, for they represent that beyond which it is impossible to see."[4]

It is not only interpreters who have horizons in this sense; the objects interpreted (if they belong to the human world) have their own horizons, "what the author accepted unquestioningly and hence did not consider." And Gadamer, famously, proposes that "understanding is always the fusion of these horizons supposedly existing by themselves."[6]

Well, not always. Sometimes we pay too little attention to the horizons of the authors we are interpreting, as when we interpret recipes from another culture, adding our own standard ingredients, which we assume must have been omitted from explicit mention because they are so obvious. ("They don't mention any garlic, but that must be because they took it for granted.") What we take for granted (our own horizon) we assume must have been taken for granted by others. In such cases, presumably, we fall short of a hermeneutical ideal that Gadamer espouses.

Our falling short of the ideal in this case can be accounted for by our heeding charity to the exclusion of the fusion of horizons. There are other cases where, conversely, we are so concerned to respect others' horizons that we attend too little to charity. Some "authentic" musical performance is like this. The interpreter imagines that all that needs to be attended to is the historical record of period performance style and, in doing so, forgets that it is still *music* that has to be performed and that there are shared understandings of what music means across historical divides. A balance of charity and fusion of horizons is desirable when we wish to assign intentional significance to an object.

The position we have arrived at regarding the attribution of intentional significance may not appear to be particularly illuminating. It just says that if you want to interpret something as the product of a human intention, then you should remember what is common between yourself and the other agent in question, while also attending to the differences between yourself and this other agent. This advice isn't going to help someone who is wondering about whether there would be anything wrong with interpreting a text or other human artifact in a way that conflicted with the stated intentions of its author. That is the issue of intentionalism, and our discussion thus far doesn't seem to help with it. Let's spend a moment on this issue.

Some philosophers believe that interpretations that accord with the author's known intentions hold a privileged position. Hirsch is one such:

> Authorial intention is not the only possible norm for interpretation, though it is the only practical norm for a cognitive discipline of interpretation. The choice of an interpretive norm is not required by the "nature of the text," but, being a choice, belongs to the domain of ethics rather than the domain of ontology.[7]

Hirsch argues in favor of this ethical choice:

> Therefore, let me state what I consider to be a fundamental ethical maxim for interpretation, a maxim that claims no privileged sanction from metaphysics or analysis, but only from general ethical tenets, generally shared. *Unless there is a powerful overriding value in disregarding an author's intention (i.e., original meaning), we who interpret as a vocation should not disregard it.* . . . Kant held it to be a foundation of moral action that men should be conceived as ends in themselves, and not as instruments of other men. This imperative is transferable to the words of men because speech is an extension and expression in the social domain, and also because when we fail to conjoin a man's intentions we lose the soul of speech, which is to convey meaning and to understand what is intended to be conveyed.[8]

Our theory obviously allows for the possibility of successful interpretations of texts that do not attribute intentional significance to those texts. Such successes occur whenever interpreters make sense of texts in ways that were unavailable to the author. So, if Hirsch is committed to the contrary position—that interpretive success is conditional upon the attribution of intentional significance to texts—we need to examine the reasoning that leads him to this position.

Hirsch's argument rests on three premises:

- an application to the case of the interpreter of the Kantian injunction against using persons instrumentally;
- a view of an author's words as extensions of the author's own self and as therefore meriting the moral consideration due to the author; and
- a view that an interpretation cannot be successful as an interpretation if it is morally defective.

All three premises should be questioned.

First, the Kantian injunction against using persons instrumentally is indeed relevant to interpreters considered as agents. It implies that interpreters, like all agents, should treat other persons, including those whose work they are interpreting, as ends in themselves, not as means. But the Kantian principle can be applied to one's attitude towards oneself as much as it applies to one's attitude towards others. So applied, it would forbid placing oneself in a position of excessive subservience in one's transactions with others, thereby allowing oneself to be used instrumentally by others. Such a consideration is relevant to the ethical situation of interpreters, whose role is to effect a transaction between themselves and the object of their interpretation. Where that object is a text or artifact, interpreters demean themselves morally if they adopt a subservient attitude to the object by attending only to the author's intentions to the exclusion of their own concerns as beings actively engaged in the enterprise of interpretation. As such, the Kantian principle seems to require of interpreters that they not allow themselves to be used as purely passive recipients of data but that they take on their active responsibilities as interpreters. In other words, the Kantian principle to which Hirsch appeals, if it shows that interpreters of texts should heed authorial intentions, doesn't show that they should heed authorial intentions to the exclusion of everything else. It also shows that interpreters should not forget their own autonomy as interpreters.

As for the second premise, Hirsch seems to be playing with the expression "the author's words." In one sense, a person's words express that person's beliefs and intentions, and to deal with them is indeed to deal with the author. In another sense, the author's words are such only in the sense that the author has created a work of art in the medium of words—a different act altogether from simply saying something. To deal with the author's words in this sense is not at all the same as dealing with the author. Texts are indeed extensions and expressions of their authors, but so are other artifacts. If words' status as extensions of the author entitled them to the same moral consideration as the authors themselves, then all artifacts would have the same status: crockery and furniture would deserve to be treated as persons. Crockery and furniture, however, are precisely the type of thing we feel ethically justified in treating as instruments to our ends. So there is no good reason to suppose that the moral consideration due to an author as a person transfers to the author's works, even if those works are expressed in the medium of words.

Finally, even if there were such a reason, there remains a further question whether morality should trump all other considerations when considering whether an interpretation succeeds or not. The possibility exists that an interpretation might succeed relative to its own aims while falling short ethically. It is not evident that interpretation's aims include any ethical content (though this is not to say that interpreters, as agents, fall outside the scope of ethics). In sum, Hirsch's reasoning does not establish that successful interpretations of texts must proceed by way of assigning intentional significance.

CHAPTER SIX

Artistic Significance

Another important type of significance is that which is attributed to objects of interpretation when we make sense of them as artistic works or performances. The significance-systems that are employed in this type of interpretation differ from ones used elsewhere, for instance in natural explanations. In natural explanations, the success of an interpretation depends on its having only laws of nature in its significance-system. In interpreting an object as having artistic significance, we rely on significance-systems drawn from the repertoire of a particular artist or school or from the conventions and traditions surrounding a particular genre or style.

The point is seemingly doubted by Robert Stecker, who, in discussing Freudian interpretations of Shakespeare, urges the question whether "there are such things as the Oedipus complex and they are among the fundamental motivators of human behavior."[9]

Actually, this question would have a bearing on the success of those Freudian interpretations only if they were reliant on the success of Freudian theory as a natural explanation of human psychology. But directors don't have to be Freudians to put on Freudian interpretations of *Hamlet*. They may do so for other reasons—for example, the fact that, true or not, such interpretations manage to make sense of the play. This they can do even if the world in which they situate the play is made up largely of falsehoods. It all depends on what style of theater is involved. If it's a theater of reason and realism, that is one thing; if it's a theater of the imagination, that is another. Stecker displays an unhealthy preoccupation with the truth and seems to overlook essential distinctions between different types of interpretation.

What, then, are the distinctive marks of artistic significance? We noted earlier that coherence is a consequence of significance, and I want to pursue the question of artistic significance by examining the nature of artistic coherence.

In 1992 Gidon Kremer and the Chamber Orchestra of Europe,

conducted by Nikolaus Harnoncourt, recorded a version of Beethoven's *Violin Concerto* incorporating a first-movement cadenza scored for violin, tympani, and offstage piano.[10] The cadenza was an arrangement by Kremer of the cadenza that Beethoven himself wrote for his own arrangement of the *Violin Concerto* for piano and orchestra. In terms of our model, the Kremer/Harnoncourt interpretation takes as its object the Beethoven concerto minus cadenza and adds the Beethoven/Kremer cadenza to this object with a view to enhancing the object's significance.

One might argue that the interpretation is unsuccessful because it is incoherent. Stylistically and in terms of instrumentation, the addition coheres poorly with the object. The piano has not been heard before this moment (some twenty minutes into the movement). On hearing the cadenza, one wonders, What is a piano doing in a violin concerto? And why is it offstage? (Is its location a sign that *behind* this version for violin and piano lies Beethoven's version for piano alone?)

In judging the cadenza to cohere poorly with the remainder of the movement, one is appealing to a notion of specifically musical coherence—perhaps even more specifically, one has in mind a kind of coherence appropriate to a violin concerto. On the other hand, those who find coherence in this rendition can point to the cadenza's origin as a work by Beethoven, designed specifically for (an arrangement of) the *Violin Concerto*. The sleeve-note writer is one of these, and he insists: "The cadenza is by Beethoven. . . . There is no question of any extension or alteration to the structure contained in the original manuscript. The only re-arrangement concerns the instrumentation."[11]

The dispute concerns the type of coherence that should be demanded of a cadenza in the Beethoven *Violin Concerto*. Further light on the dispute can perhaps be gained by noting that coherence of a set of elements depends on the degree of connectedness among those elements. Clearly, a set of elements might be judged to be lacking in coherence even while exhibiting a high degree of connectedness, provided that the disconnected elements were sufficiently important. The Beethoven/Kremer cadenza is connected to the rest of the movement through its composer and its original designation for a place in the (arranged) *Violin Concerto*; it is disconnected by virtue of its instrumentation and (to some extent) its style. The cadenza's connection to the rest of the movement through its composer and its original designation for a place in the (arranged) *Violin Concerto* is not something that can be heard, though it is something that can be known, for instance by a musicologist. The instrumentation and style, unlike the fact that Beethoven wrote the music originally for an arrangement of the concerto, are audible features of the cadenza. Their audibility is crucial to the question of whether they should feature in the interpretation of the work-plus-cadenza as art, because art has to be able to be experienced. Therefore, in this case, it seems that the sleeve-note writer's interpretation, while successful as a piece of musicology, does not warrant the insertion of the cadenza into an artistic performance of the work. Those of us for whom the concerto is primarily an artistic listening experience may justly conclude that the cadenza's auditory disconnectedness with the rest of the movement is more important that its historical connectedness. Richard Wollheim emphasizes this experiential aspect of interpreting artworks:

> That the process of understanding a work of art—and here the natural contrast is with understanding an utterance or an inscription—is essentially experiential is clearly recognized when we think that to change one's mind about the meaning of a work of art simply on the basis of retailed evidence without perceptual return to the work itself is illegitimate.[12]

TYPES OF REPRESENTATIONAL SUITABILITY

It is not demanded of a successful interpretation that it cover absolutely everything about its object, only those elements that are picked up in the object-as-represented. Consequently, we can distinguish types of comprehensiveness according to the types of sets of elements that are to be covered. For example, in interpreting Plato's dialogues, which elements in the text are we to take as the object of our interpretation? On one view, it is only the *arguments* in the text that are a fit object of philosophical interpretation. On another view, there are many other elements of the text that must be accounted for in a satisfactory interpretation—the dramatic context, the location, the illocutionary force of individual speeches. Comprehensiveness comes to different things for these two types of Platonic interpretation.

Comprehensiveness of the representation, as of the governing concept, is a matter of degree, in the following sense. Given that the features of the object (or the object-as-represented) can be enumerated, then—relative to some such enumeration—one interpretation is more comprehensive than another if it takes into account more of those features than does its rival. But of course in practice there will always be more than one way of individuating an object's features.

In order for an interpretation to encompass the whole of the object, two conditions must be met: the governing concept must fit the object-as-represented, both its content and the mode of representation, and the representation must be a suitable one, in the sense that the governing concept is such that if it applies to the object-as-represented, then it will apply to the object.

This second condition—that the governing concept be such that if it applies to the object-as-represented, then it applies to the object—can be satisfied in one of two ways. The object may be taken as a given, along with its features; its representation may then turn out to be such as to preserve all of the object's features that are relevant so far as the governing concept is concerned. Alternatively, the representation may be taken as a given, and its features may be taken as defining the object's features; in which case, of course, it becomes true that if the governing concept applies to the object-as-represented it thereby applies to the object. Let's look more closely at these two types of suitability.

CHAPTER SIX

An interesting case where the suitability of interpretive representation becomes an issue is the Leiber-Stoller song "Hound Dog."[13] This was first recorded in 1952 by Willie Mae "Big Mama" Thornton.[14] The drift of the song's lyrics is well conveyed by Jerry Leiber in an interview with David Fricke for *Rolling Stone*:

> We saw Big Mama and she knocked me cold. She looked like the biggest, baddest, saltyist chick you would ever see. And she was mean, a "lady bear" as they used to call 'em. She must have been 350 lbs and she had all these scars all over her face. I had to write a song for her that basically said "Go fuck yourself" but how do you do it without actually saying it? And how do you do it telling a story? I couldn't just have a song full of expletives, hence the "Hound Dog."[15]

Presley's 1956 version alters the lyrics. Only the first line and the general verse form are the same in the two versions. Not even the subject matter of the original verse has been retained in the Presley version; what was a harangue against a former lover seems to have become a diatribe against a delinquent dog. Presley also includes a line, not in the original, deploring the dog's inefficiency as a rabbit catcher. Jerry Leiber comments, "That version of the lyric didn't make any sense."[16]

But these changes are as nothing when compared with the way Elvis transforms the music from rhythm and blues into rock and roll. Elvis's version is much faster and has a nervous quality altogether lacking in the original. One critic writes of the music's "driving rhythm," "pumping energy," its "gutty, raunchy sound," describing it as "one continual blast."[17]

Then there is Elvis's *performance*:

> With Milton Berle, Elvis was to achieve the wildest success ever before on live camera, cutting loose with *Hound Dog*, and performing it with more defiance and sexuality than ever on television. With the drums driving across the song, Elvis's body jolted, his shoulders jerked, the hips and groin gyrated to the screams of the live audience and especially of the young audience across America.[18]

What do these changes signify? Samuel Roy interprets them as follows:

> *Hound Dog* is not just a piece of music from a cultural revolution of the 1950s; it stands for much more than that. The song essentially states that it's time to become the aggressor. *Hound Dog* was a turning point, primarily because of what it stood for. The point was not that Elvis dared to rock, but that he dared to express disdain for cultural and social pressures that bound and imprisoned the youth within themselves.[19]

(Notice that the "Hound Dog" he is talking about is *Elvis's* "Hound Dog.")

Greil Marcus proposes another interpretation. Alice Walker, in her short story "Nineteen Fifty-Five," portrays a white pop singer who buys a song from a black woman, makes his name with it, and then spends the rest of life wondering what the song means.[20] The story has been read as a parable about Big Mama, Elvis, and "Hound Dog." The point of the parable is summarized by Marcus:

> It's an argument about the nature of American culture: about how white America was sold, and happily bought, a bill of goods, and about how black America was bilked. The white boy robs the black woman—pay her, yes, dutifully, piously, even, but some things can never be paid for—and dies of guilt.

Marcus's language makes it clear that he rejects the parable as an interpretation of the history of "Hound Dog." He sees it as fitting "neatly into various cultural prejudices, some of which are those of American blacks, and more of which are those of white middle-class Americans." More importantly, Marcus cannot accept the idea that a rendition as original as Elvis's "Hound Dog" was based on a misunderstanding.[21] Marcus rightly emphasizes the unique significance of Elvis's "Hound Dog," and also its mysteriousness: "That Elvis did what he did—and we do not know precisely what he did, because 'Milkcow Blues Boogie' and

'Hound Dog' cannot be figured out, exactly—means that the world became something other than what it would have been had he not done what he did."²²

It strikes me as a distinct possibility that Elvis didn't understand the song. It is in no way ruled out by the originality of his recording. In fact, the originality of Elvis's version might be partly *explained* by its being a misunderstanding of the original. In any case—whether or not it is a misunderstanding of the song—Elvis's version is a *misreading* of it (assuming it is a reading at all). And the question is, Was this misreading a suitable representation of the song, relative to Elvis's interpretive aims?

This question could be answered either way, depending on what we take to be the referent of the name "Hound Dog." If that name refers to the original song, then it is not true that Elvis's governing concept "rock number" is such that if it is true of his representation of the song, then it is true of the song. The reason is that, while Elvis's representation is a rock number, the original song isn't; so the representation is not suitable. On the other hand, one might say "Hound Dog" has *become* a rock and roll number in Elvis's hands. Nicholas Barber seems to think so: "Nowadays it's impossible to think of 'Hound Dog' without thinking of [Elvis's] name."²³

And recall the way Samuel Roy *meant* Elvis's version in speaking of "Hound Dog." If one is happy to speak in this way, one is committed to saying that an interpretation (albeit a flawed one) can alter its object—it can establish a new version of its text.²⁴ Objects of interpretation may (in Margolis's terms) have histories rather than natures.²⁵ And in that case—if the name "Hound Dog" refers to what the song has *now become*—then Elvis's is after all a suitable representation of the song—not of the song in its old form but in the new form, of which Elvis was a coauthor.²⁶ His governing concept "rock number" is such that if it is true of his representation of the song, then it is true of the song. The reason is that his representation has come to *define* the song.

Is this result shocking? How can it be possible for the interpreter to change the identity of the object of interpretation? The answer is that this is possible if there is no requirement of data priority. But of course, even if it's possible, it's not *easy* to do what Elvis did with "Hound Dog."

Did Elvis get "Hound Dog" wrong, or did "Hound Dog" become something different in Elvis's hands? Both are true. Taking intentional objects to be sets of features (augmented by sets of beliefs), what we call "a song." taken as an intentional object, can have a history. The set of features that at one time is taken to identify the song can develop into a different set of identifying features at a later time. It's the same with stories, as Stan Godlovitch observes: "The identity of the legend, story or character is profoundly flexible; hence, a story may evolve over time. This could be crucial in keeping the story alive for later generations."[27]

The transformations by means of which intentional objects such as songs and stories change over time include misinterpretations as well as interpretations. What is crucial is that the (mis)interpretation be so persuasive as to carry conviction and thereby to supplant earlier renditions; this is not just a matter of different "covers" of the same song, but of the song changing over time. In this way, "Hound Dog" became something different in Elvis's hands. However, even if an intentional object undergoes development over time, the *external* object that originally corresponded to it might remain unchanged. In this way, the Leiber-Stoller song has not changed, and Elvis got "Hound Dog" wrong.

NOTES

1. Paul Thagard, *Conceptual Revolutions* (Princeton: Princeton University Press, 1992), 68.
2. Simon Blackburn, *The Oxford Dictionary of Philosophy* (Oxford: Oxford University Press, 1994), 62.
3. Blackburn, *Oxford Dictionary of Philosophy*, 178.
4. Hans-Georg Gadamer, *Truth and Method*, trans.Joel Weinsheimer and Donald G. Marshall, 2d ed. (New York: Continuum, 1994), 306.

5. Gadamer, *Truth and Method*, 374.
6. Gadamer, *Truth and Method*, 306.
7. E. D. Hirsch Jr., *The Aims of Interpretation* (Chicago: University of Chicago Press, 1976), 7.
8. Hirsch, *Aims*, 90.
9. Robert Stecker, *Artworks: Definition, Meaning, Value* (University Park: Pennsylvania State University Press, 1997), 140–41.
10. Ludwig von Beethoven, *Violin Concerto*, Gidon Kremer and the Chamber Orchestra of Europe, Nikolaus Harnoncourt, TELDEC 9031-74881-2.
11. Wolf-Eberhard von Lewinski, liner notes to TELDEC 9031-74881-2.
12. Richard Wollheim, "Art, Interpretation, and Perception," in *The Mind and Its Depths* (Cambridge: Harvard University Press, 1993), 142.
13. *Presley: The All-Time Greatest Hits*, RCA ND90100.
14. *Big Mama Thornton: The Original Hound Dog*, Peacock Ace CDCHD940. There is also a 1975 version of Thornton singing this number (*Big Mama Thornton: Jail*, Vanguard 79351-2).
15. Quoted in Ray Topping's liner notes to *The Original Hound Dog*, Ace Records CDCHD 940.
16. Quoted in Topping, liner notes to *Original Hound Dog*.
17. Samuel Roy, *Elvis: Prophet of Power* (Brookline, Mass.: Branden, 1985), 13–14.
18. Roy, *Elvis*, 18.
19. Roy, *Elvis*, 15.
20. See Alice Walker, "Nineteen Fifty-Five," in *You Can't Keep a Good Woman Down* (New York: Harcourt Brace Jovanovich, 1981), 3–20.
21. Greil Marcus, *Dead Elvis: A Chronicle of a Cultural Obsession* (Harmondsworth, England: Penguin Books, 1991), 36–37.
22. Marcus, *Dead Elvis*, 8.
23. Nicholas Barber, "Hound Dog," in *Lives of the Great Songs*, ed. Tim de Lisle (Harmondsworth, England: Penguin Books, 1995), 202–7, 202.
24. It is a further question whether an interpretation that is *not* flawed can do so.
25. Joseph Margolis, *Interpretation Radical but Not Unruly: The New Puzzle of the Arts and History* (Berkeley and Los Angeles: University of California Press, 1995), 7.
26. Umberto Eco (*The Limits of Interpretation*, 62) might say that Elvis's is a *use* rather than an interpretation of the song.
27. Stan Godlovitch, *Musical Performance: A Philosophical Study* (London: Routledge, 1998), 93.

7

CONCLUSIONS

Let's return to the problems we identified in chapter 1 and see how our theory of interpretation deals with them.

PLURALISM

If, in the nature of the case, interpretation goes beyond its object by supplying representations and conceptualizations that are not implicit in the object itself, it's clear that there can be many interpretations of a single object. Beyond that, Krausz makes the point that a pluralism (or, as he says, "multiplism") with regard to ideally admissible interpretations is not entailed by the fact that objects underdetermine their interpretations. So we still need to ask, Can there be several *successful* interpretations of the same object?

Yes: so far as concerns their general conditions of success, two interpretations of a Beethoven symphony—say, by Toscanini and Hogwood—might be equally successful. This is not surprising, because these two interpreters have different aims: one aims to present Beethoven's music on modern instruments in an "objective" but highly charged style, the other to present the music on original instruments in a style that emphasizes links with Beethoven's eighteenth-century (distinctly un-Toscaninian) predecessors. To an extent, therefore, the two are incommensurable, since they have different aims. If they had had the same aims, Toscanini's interpretation could have been compared with Hogwood's and been found to be less successful in its attainment of those aims.

A further, more substantial, question suggests itself. Could there be a plurality of interpretations, each of which satisfies the general constraints on interpretation, and all having all terms in common—the same governing concept and representation, as well as the same object? The answer to this question seems to be no; it seems that any salient difference between interpretations must be able to be construed as a difference in one of these terms, otherwise our list of interpretation's terms would not be complete. To the extent that all salient features of interpretation can be resumed under the terms we identified in chapter 2, it seems that interpretations differing in a salient feature must also differ in one or more of their terms.

This, however, is not quite correct. It is a corollary of our account of the general conditions for success in interpretation that if the governing concept in a successful interpretation is replaced by a more general concept, the resulting interpretation will also be successful. From this corollary it follows that one successful interpretation could differ from another solely by having a more general governing concept, all other terms being shared. This being so, it seems that one successful interpretation could differ from another solely by having a different governing concept, provided that both governing concepts were subsumed under a single more general concept.

Two performances of the same music by the same artist might be seen as executing a single ongoing interpretation governed by a single governing concept. They might also, in a different way, be seen as exhibiting salient differences. But to the extent that the two performances are seen as embodying distinct interpretations, we can construe them as governed by two distinct concepts, both of which are subsumed under the more general concept that governs the artist's ongoing interpretation of the music. Our earlier example of Horowitz's Liszt sonata confirms this and suggests a negative answer to the substantial question of interpretive pluralism: there are no divergent successful interpretations with identical terms.

Success, however, is not the same as value. Success may indeed be valued, but so may other attributes. Toscanini's Beethoven is valued not just for its success but for its energy, attack, excitement, and punch. Hogwood's is valued for its instrumental timbres, characteristic tempi, and historical accuracy. Both are valued for their integrity and clarity. Sometimes what succeeds is not valued at all and what doesn't succeed is valued highly. (Recall Tanner on the *Ring*.) We are thus led to ask whether there could be equally valuable interpretations of the same object.

Michael Krausz argues for a positive answer:

> What is specified in a score . . . is not sufficient for an ideally admissible interpretation of it. Extra-score practices are required for completing the interpretation. Since these practices may vary, and no one of them can be established as the single right one, the view that there is a single right musical interpretation must yield to the view that there may be a multiplicity of ideally admissible interpretations. Where there are no univocal and overarching standards in virtue of which one may say that one among a number of interpretation practices is conclusively better than another, there can be no single ideal musical interpretation.[1]

The point seems unanswerable in the case of musical interpretation. Toscanini's and Hogwood's Beethoven are ultimately incommensurable despite the fact that there are qualities for which both are valued. Is Toscaninian electricity better or worse than Hogwoodian authenticity? If we are asked, we can only gape.

It is evident, therefore, not only that there can be several successful interpretations of the same object but also that it may be possible rationally to prefer one of them over its rivals, either because of its comparative success as an interpretation or because of some other valuable quality that it possesses.

CHAPTER SEVEN

UNIVOCITY

Annette Barnes poses the question "whether the interpreting done by critics in the various arts consists of multiple activities or of a single activity with multiple types of object."[2] Her answer is that critical interpreting consists of multiple activities. Thus she denies that even critical interpretations all belong to a single kind. She does think that critical interpretation can occur only where knowledge is lacking and that these activities share certain features: "The person engaged in them is thinking, is classifying, is able to give reasons for his classifications."[3]

But she doesn't claim that all such thinking is interpretation.[4] My own view is that all critical interpretation, along with very many other types, should be included in a single theory of interpretation, all exhibiting the structure I have described.

Hirsch expresses the hope that his idea of a corrigible schema will be "not just ecumenical but also illuminating"[5] in showing that "all cognition is analogous to interpretation."[6] I think that this conclusion is too weak. All cognition involves interpretation. Hirsch is obliged to skirt this bolder statement because of his attachment to the doctrine that interpretation always aims to discern intentions.

I have outlined a structure that I claim is found in all types of interpretation—the scientist's interpretation as much as the critic's, the performer's as much as the exegete's, the poet's as much as the rabbi's. The differences between these types arise from differences in the object (nature or art), the medium of representation (discourse or action), the point of the representation (understanding or imaginative development), and the kind of governing concept (explanation, representation, expression, etc.). If this is right, then our answer to the question of univocity is yes: all interpretation exhibits the same structure, that is, there is a single set of functions to be performed in any operation of interpretation, even though what performs these functions varies from one kind of interpretation to another.

CONCLUSIONS

COMPATIBILITY

Our three-tier structure—object, object-as-represented, and governing concept—allows us simultaneously to maintain the principle of pluralism and that of the hermeneutic circle, given a modified version of the hermeneutic circle that states that if the interpretation is different, then the object-*as-represented* is different. One and the same object can have several interpretations, even if one and the same object-as-represented can't, provided that one and the same object can be represented in several ways. So pluralism is compatible with the modified hermeneutic circle. To this extent, the three-tier structure provides us with a way of preserving both our principles.

By contrast, if we stuck to a two-tier structure consisting just of the object and its interpretation, then we couldn't maintain *both* the hermeneutic circle *and* pluralism. We can't maintain pluralism along with DIDO, since DIDO tells us that if there are several interpretations, then there are several objects.

THEORY AS INTERPRETATION

Finally, I come back to the question whether what we have been engaged in is itself interpretation. Is theory interpretation? Well, the answer to which we are committed is that if theory exhibits the three-tier structure we have attributed to interpretation, then it too is interpretation. And what we have been engaged in *does* exhibit that structure.

I started by listing data that any theory would have to account for; that was the object of our interpretation. I went on to show a systematic way of representing those data in terms of a three-tier structure; that was the object-as-represented. Finally, I constructed a conceptual framework that made sense of the data. It should come as no surprise to us at the end of our inquiry that we ourselves are interpreters of interpreters.

If I am right about the nature of interpretation, then the question of whether the theory put forward in these pages is itself better or worse than other accounts of the matter comes down to two questions:

- Does the theory put forward here make better sense of the phenomena of interpretation than do rival accounts?

- Does the theory cover the phenomena comprehensively?

The theory appears to be comprehensive. It purports to cover all the types of interpretation that are commonly recognized. Whether it *makes sense* of all these phenomena, however, may be disputed. Some critics will say it doesn't make much sense of the phenomena, because it relies so heavily on this very phrase "making sense"—a phrase, they will say, that is hopelessly ambiguous and doesn't pick out a unified concept. The reader must judge whether comprehensiveness has in this instance been gained at the cost of intelligibility.

NOTES

1. Michael Krausz, *Rightness and Reasons: Interpretation in Cultural Practices* (Ithaca, N.Y.: Cornell University Press, 1993), 22.
2. Annette Barnes, *On Interpretation: A Critical Analysis* (Oxford: Basil Blackwell, 1988), 159.
3. Barnes, *On Interpretation*, 165.
4. See Barnes, *On Interpretation*, chap. 8.
5. E. D. Hirsch Jr., *The Aims of Interpretation* (Chicago: University of Chicago Press, 1976), 34–35.
6. Hirsch, *Aims*, 32.

BIBLIOGRAPHY

Barber, Nicholas. "Hound Dog." In *Lives of the Great Songs*, edited by Tim de Lisle, 202–7. Harmondsworth, England: Penguin Books, 1995.

Barnes, Annette. *On Interpretation: A Critical Analysis*. Oxford: Basil Blackwell, 1988.

Barthes, Roland. "From Work to Text." In *The Rustle of Language*. Translated by Richard Howard, 56–64. New York: Blackwell, 1986.

Bartholomeusz, Dennis. *The Winter's Tale in Performance in England and America 1611–1976*. Cambridge: Cambridge University Press, 1982.

Blackburn, Simon. *The Oxford Dictionary of Philosophy*. Oxford: Oxford University Press, 1994.

Bloom, Harold. *The Western Canon: The Books and School of the Ages*. London: Papermac, 1995.

Bonjour, Laurence. *The Structure of Empirical Knowledge*. Cambridge: Harvard University Press, 1985.

Bradley, F. H. *Essays on Truth and Reality*. Oxford: Clarendon Press, 1914.

Currie, Gregory. *Image and Mind: Film, Philosophy, and Cognitive Science*. Cambridge: Cambridge University Press, 1995.

Dean, Winton. *Handel's Dramatic Oratorios and Masques*. London: Oxford University Press, 1959.

Deutsch, Otto Erich. *Mozart: A Documentary Biography*. Translated by Eric Blom, Peter Branscombe, and Jeremy Noble. 2d ed. London: Adam & Charles Black, 1966.

Dickie, George. "Definition of 'Art.'" In *A Companion to Aesthetics*, edited by David E. Cooper, 109–13. Oxford: Basil Blackwell, 1992.

Eco, Umberto. *The Limits of Interpretation*. Bloomington: Indiana University Press, 1990.

———. "Reply." In *Interpretation and Overinterpretation*, edited by Stefan Collini. 139–51. Cambridge: Cambridge University Press, 1992.

Fodor, Jerry A. "Observation Reconsidered." In *A Theory of Content and Other Essays*, 231–52. Cambridge: MIT Press, 1990.

Gadamer, Hans-Georg. *Truth and Method*. Translated by Joel Weinsheimer and Donald G. Marshall. 2d ed. New York: Continuum, 1994.

Godlovitch, Stan. *Musical Performance: A Philosophical Study*. London: Routledge, 1998.

Goodman, Nelson. "Variations on Variation—Or Picasso Back to Bach." In *Reconceptions in Philosophy and Other Arts and Sciences*, by Nelson Goodman and Catherine Z. Elgin, 66–82. London: Routledge, 1988.

Handel, *Eracle*, Orchestra e Coro del Teatro alla Scala. Lovro von Matacic. Giuseppe Di Stefano Records GDS 3001(3). Liner notes by Guiseppe di Stefano.

Hardy, Phil, and Dave Laing. *The Faber Companion to Twentieth-Century Popular Music*. Rev. ed. London: Faber & Faber, 1995.

Hirsch, E. D., Jr., *Validity in Interpretation*. New Haven: Yale University Press, 1967.

———. *The Aims of Interpretation*. Chicago: University of Chicago Press, 1976.

Hopkins, Antony. *Understanding Music*. London: J. M. Dent, 1979.

Horowitz, Vladimir. *Horowitz Plays Liszt*. RCA Victor Red Seal 09026 61415 2.

———. *Recordings 1930–1951*. EMI MONO CHS 7 63538 2.

Hutcheson, Linda. *A Theory of Parody: The Teachings of Twentieth-Century Art Forms*. New York: Methuen, 1985.

Johnson, Douglas. Liner notes to Beethoven, *Piano Concertos nos. 3 and 4*. Melvyn Tan and the London Classical Players. Roger Norrington. EMI, 1989 CDC 7 49815 2.

Kellner, Douglas. "Madonna, Fashion, and Identity." In *On Fashion*, edited by Shari Benstock and Suzanne Ferriss, 159–82. New Brunswick, N.J.: Rutgers University Press, 1994.

Kivy, Peter. *The Corded Shell: Reflections on Musical Expression*. Princeton, N.J.: Princeton University Press, 1980.

———. *Authenticities: Philosophical Reflections on Musical Performance*. Ithaca, N.Y.: Cornell University Press, 1995.

Kleczynski, Jan. *Chopin's Greater Works*. Translated by Natalie Janota. London: William Reeves, 1896.

Krausz, Michael. *Rightness and Reasons: Interpretation in Cultural Practices*. Ithaca, N.Y.: Cornell University Press, 1993.

Kuhn, Thomas S. "The Natural and the Human Sciences." In *The Interpretive Turn: Philosophy, Science, Culture*, edited by David R. Hiley, James F. Bohman, and Richard Shusterman, 17–24. Ithaca, N.Y.: Cornell University Press, 1991.

Lee, Peggy. *Twenty-Four Great Songs*. Personality PRS 23012. Anonymous liner notes.

Levinson, Jerrold. "Performative versus Critical Interpretations in Music." In *The Interpretation of Music: Philosophical Essays*, edited by Michael Krausz, 33–60. Oxford: Clarendon Press, 1993.

Leys, Simon. *The Analects of Confucius*. New York: W. W. Norton, 1997.

Lindenberger, Herbert. *Opera in History from Monteverdi to Cage*. Stanford, Calif.: Stanford University Press, 1998.

Lubin, Albert. *Stranger on the Earth: A Psychological Biography of Vincent Van Gogh*. New York: Holt, Reinhart & Winston, 1972.

Madonna. *The Girlie Show, Live Down Under*. Warner Reprise 7599383913. Video.

Marcus, Greil. *Dead Elvis: A Chronicle of a Cultural Obsession*. Harmondsworth, England: Penguin Books, 1992.

Margolis, Joseph. *Art and Philosophy.* Brighton: Harvester, 1980.

———. "Hermeneutics." In *A Companion to Aesthetics*, edited by David E. Cooper, 192–97. Oxford: Blackwell, 1992.

———. *Interpretation Radical but Not Unruly: The New Puzzle of the Arts and History.* Berkeley and Los Angeles: University of California Press, 1995.

Nietzsche, Friederich. *The Will to Power.* Translated by Walter Kaufmann and R. J. Honingdale. London: Weidenfeld & Nicolson, 1968.

Orga, Ates, and Nikolai Demidenko. Liner notes to Frédéric-François Chopin, *The Four Scherzi.* Nikolai Demidenko. Hyperion CDA66514, 1991.

Plantinga, Alvin. *Warrant: The Current Debate.* New York: Oxford University Press, 1993.

Plato. *Ion.* Translated by Lane Cooper. In *The Collected Dialogues of Plato Including the Letters*, edited by Edith Hamilton and Huntington Cairns, 215–28. New York: Pantheon Books, 1961.

Presley, Elvis. *The All-Time Greatest Hits.* RCA ND9000.

Rosen, Charles. *The Classical Style.* London: Faber & Faber, 1971.

Roy, Samuel. *Elvis: Prophet of Power.* Brookline, Mass.: Branden, 1985.

Schleiermacher, F. D. E. *Hermeneutik.* Edited by Heinz Kimmerle. Heidelberg: C. Winter, 1959.

Schonberg, Harold C. *Horowitz: His Life and Music.* New York: Simon & Schuster, 1992.

Schulze, Laurie, Anne Barton White, and Jane D. Brown. "'A Sacred Monster in Her Prime': Audience Construction of Madonna as Low-Other." In *The Madonna Connection: Representational Politics, Subcultural Identities, and Cultural Theory*, edited by Cathy Schwichtenberg, 15–37. Sydney: Allen & Unwin, 1993.

Sophocles. *Trachiniae.* Edited by P. E. Easterling. Cambridge: Cambridge University Press, 1982.

Stecker, Robert. *Artworks: Definition, Meaning, Value.* University Park: Pennsylvania State University Press, 1997.

Tanner, Michael. *Wagner.* London: Flamingo, 1997.

Tetzlaff, David. "Metatextual Girl." In *The Madonna Connection*, edited by Cathy Scheichtenberg, 239–64. Boulder, Colo.: Westview Press, 1993.

Thagard, Paul. *Conceptual Revolutions.* Princeton, N.J.: Princeton University Press, 1992.

Thornton, Big Mama. *The Original Hound Dog.* Peacock Ace CDCHD940. Liner notes by Ray Topping.

Von Lewinski, Wolf-Eberhard. Liner notes to Beethoven, Ludwig, *Violin Concerto, Romances.* Chamber Orchestra of Europe. Nikolaus Harnoncourt. TELDEC 9031-74881-2.

Walker, Alice. "Nineteen Fifty-Five." In *You Can't Keep A Good Woman Down*, 3–20. London: Women's Press, 1982.

Whewell, W. *Of Induction, with Especial Reference to Mr. J. Stuart Mill's System of Logic.* London: John W. Parker, 1849.

Wollheim, Richard. "Art, Interpretation, and Perception." In *The Mind and Its Depth*, 132–43. Cambridge: Harvard University Press, 1993.

INDEX

allusion, 9
applicatio, 55–56
arrangement, 65
Ave Maria (Bach/Gounod), 46

Barber, Nicholas, 100
Barnes, Annette, 106
Barthes, Roland, 11
Bartholomeusz, Daniel, 42
Belshazzar, 37–38
Bloom, Harold, 81
Bonjour, Laurence, 76–77
Borges, Jorge Luis, 15
Bradley, F. H., 21
Bremmer, H. P., 40

charity, principle of, 89–90
Chopin, Frederic, 43–45
coherence, 8, 25, 73–79, 84–85, 94–96
comprehensiveness, 12, 73, 79–81, 83–85, 97, 108
concept, governing, 19–20, 22, 28, 31–32, 35, 37–47, 53, 55–56, 63–68, 79, 84, 97, 107
conceptualization, 19, 28–30, 31, 37, 79–80

consilience, 80–81
contextualization, 25, 31, 66
correction, 41–42
critical monism, 13
Currie, Gregory, 15–16
cutting, 42–43

Daniel, 37
data, and difficulties, 3, 8, 107
Dean, Winton, 27
Demidenko, Nikolai, 44, 63
di Stefano, Giuseppe, 27
Dickie, George, 15–16
DIDO (different interpretation, different object), 10, 13–14, 17, 107
Dilthey, Wilhelm, 48

Eco, Umberto, 14, 74–76
enthymeme, 38
Europeras 1 & 2 (Cage), 72–73
explanation. *See* interpretation: and explanation

Fever (Blackwell), 45–47, 62
First Symphony (Beethoven), 41–42
Fodor, Jerry, 8–9

INDEX

Fourth Piano Concerto (Beethoven), 58–60
Freud, Sigmund, 81

Gadamer, Hans-Georg, 56, 90
Garrick, David, 42–43
genre, 25, 39
Godlovitch, Stan, 101
Goodman, Nelson, 66
Graetz, H. R., 40

Hercules (Handel), 5–6, 19, 21, 27–28, 73
hermeneutic circle, principle of, 14–17, 47–48, 107
hermeneutics, 2–3, 6–7
Hirsch, E. D., 10–11, 13–14, 25, 36, 38–39, 47–48, 55–56, 91–93, 106
Heidegger, Martin, 48
horizons, fusion of, 89–90
Horowitz, Vladimir, 31–32, 105
Hound Dog, 98–101
Hutcheson, Linda, 66

interpretation: adequational, 16–17, 39–41; adoption of, 12, 48–49; aims of, 25, 71–81, 103–4; of art, 7, 11, 54, 94–96; articulation of, 12; conscious and unconscious, 9; constructive, 12, 16–17, 39–47, 68, 88; critical, 11, 15, 53, 54, 57–64, 74, 106; of the cultural, 7–8, 53; evaluation of, 2, 3, 71–101; of experience, 7, 60, 85, 96; and explanation, 2, 8, 15–16, 38, 53, 67–68, 82–83, 87–89, 94; kinds of, 2, 3, 53–68; method of, 2, 3, 85; nature of, 2, 8–9, 11, 20; of nature, 8, 10, 53, 54, 67, 80, 87–89; object of, 14–15, 20–26, 35–37, 53–54, 56–68, 79–80, 82–83, 89, 107; as operation, 14, 19–20, 30–32, 36; partial, 13; of past, 6, 9, 54; performative, 11, 12, 15, 32, 53, 54, 56–63, 78; plurality of, 2, 10–11, 12–13, 103–5; as process, 2, 3, 35, 39, 47–48, 85; rules of, 3–4, 84; of self, 3, 7, 9, 49; the single best, 10–11, 91; statements about and statements expressing, 11–12; and understanding, 2, 68; univocity of, 15–16, 106
interpretations, combinable, 11–13, 22

Kellner, Douglas, 46
King Lear (Shakespeare), 11
Kivy, Peter, 62, 65
Kleczynski, Jan, 60
Krausz, Michael, 40–42, 103, 105
Kremer, Gidon, 94–96
Kuhn, Thomas, 36

Lavoisier, Antoine-Laurent, 8, 67, 73, 78
Lee, Peggy, 45
Leiber, Jerry, 98
Levinson, Jerrold, 56–62
Lindenberger, Herbert, 66–67
Lubin, Albert, 64

Macbeth, Lady, 81
Madonna, 45–47, 62
Magic Flute, The (Mozart), 23–25, 78, 80
Marcus, Greil, 99
Margolis, Joseph, 7–8, 16–17, 83–84, 100
meteorology, ancient, 36, 42, 82
Muller-Lyer illusion, 8–9

INDEX

natural kinds, 13
Nietzsche, Friedrich, 14

object: appropriate, 82; external, 20; local and global, 21–26, 78–81
object-as-represented, 27, 28, 48, 79, 83–84, 96–97, 107
Orfeo (Gluck), 59–60
Orga, Ates, 44, 63
oxygen, 8, 67, 73

parody, 9, 66–68
Piaget, Jean, 38
Plantinga, Alvin, 76–77
Plato, 1, 37, 39
pluralism, principle of, 10, 17, 107
Potato Eaters, The (Van Gogh), 40–41, 64
Presley, Elvis, 98–101

quotation, 9, 28

reconstitution, 43–47
relativism, 17
repetition, 9, 28
representation, 19–20, 26–28, 30–32, 35, 39–47, 53–54, 56–63, 79, 83; suitable, 81, 83–84, 96–101
restructuring, 40
Rigoletto, 30
Ring cycle (Wagner), 7, 74–76, 79, 84–85, 105
Roy, Samuel, 99–100

Schleiermacher, F. D. E., 22
Schonberg, Harold C., 31
significance, 28–30, 35, 37, 38, 55–56, 65–66, 72–79, 82–84, 87–96; artistic, 94–96; intentional, 88–93; natural explanatory, 87–89
significance-system, 29–30, 31, 63, 67, 83, 87–88, 94
simplicity, 8, 73
Stecker, Robert, 11–14, 94
summary, 10

Tanner, Michael, 7, 74–76, 79, 84, 105
Tetzlaff, David, 45
Thagard, Paul, 73, 88
Thales, 37
theory, 1–2, 107–8
Third Ballade (Chopin), 60
Thornton, Willie Mae "Big Mama," 98–99

understanding. *See* interpretation: and understanding

variation, 10, 66
versions, 12, 65
Violin Concerto (Beethoven), 94–96

Walker, Alice, 99
Whewell, William, 80
Winter's Tale (Shakespeare), 42
Wollheim, Richard, 96

ABOUT THE AUTHOR

Paul Thom is dean of arts at the Australian National University. His publications include *For an Audience: A Philosophy of the Performing Arts* (Temple University Press, 1993) as well as two books on the history of logic: *The Syllogism* (Philosophia, 1981) and *The Logic of Essentialism: An Interpretation of Aristotle's Model Syllogistic* (Kluwer, 1996). He plays the harpsichord and has worked as an opera director, staging four of Handel's dramatic oratorios.

www.ingramcontent.com/pod-product-compliance
Lightning Source LLC
Chambersburg PA
CBHW030117010526
44116CB00005B/289